My Friend Bob Jones I and my wife had the honor of being able to spend over 7 years almost daily spending time with Bob. We traveled together and I listened to his stories of the Lord moving in mighty ways during his life. For almost every Wed. I sat in his living room listing and learning. Many have asked me "did you get his mantel when he passed", and they just don't understand he was my friend and not one that I was looking for something. I was with him in very low times and high times, but always he maintained his focus on the Lord. I took notes for over 7 years and decided that his words, and stories will always have meaning in my life, and hopefully in yours...So I created this collection of experiences he had to honor his words and testimonies

D1417799

Fire Side Chats With Bob Jones

Published by **Steve Lappin**

HOW IT ALL STARTED

He called me his Jewish chauffeur and Janis his upstairs maid.....I was honored to be his friend. For over seven years I sat at his feet with others and was washed by the fountain of God's Word. Bob went home to be with the Lord Feb 14, 2014 Valentines Day. His over all message was. "Did you learn to Love?"" These are words and Testimonies I heard from 1998-2007....... His words and Testimonies are an encouragement today.

One of Bob's prayer for the Body of Christ.

"In Jesus name, I do bless you. And let your eyes open to see that love will enter into you and have His perfect work in you and bring you to that place so you'll be a vessel of love poured out to all who come your way. In Jesus name, amen."

HOW IT ALL STARTED..MY RELATIONSHIP WITH BOB AND HIS MOVE TO NC

It was April 1995 and Janis and I went to a Morningstar conf. This was the beginning of the Lord showing us that we would be moving from NY to Charlotte. Steve Lappin had a prophetic experience in 1995. He and his wife, Janis went for ministry, and Aaron Evans and Randy Cutter spoke prophetic words to them, and one of the words was "I see you sitting at the feet of Bob Jones, and waiting on him". Steve had never met Bob Jones, but had seen him once in NY at a conf. where a lot of miracles took place. At the conf. after receiving this word Steve's antenna was up during the meetings. Bob and his wife Viola were sitting up front. Steve felt the Lord pushing him with a word for Bob. Steve was holding back and the meeting was over and he just sat about five rows from where Bob was. All of a sudden Bob turned in his seat and starred at Steve. Steve knew he had to go over to him, and walked up to him where people were coming up to him and wanting him to bless them. There was a vacant seat on one side of him, and he grabbed Steve's arm and pulled him into the chair with his head landing on his chest. As he waited for the line to come to an end he listened to Bob give words of comfort and hope to those who came up. After all had finished I leaned over and said I believe the Lord gave me a word for you. He said what is it. I said the Lord wants you to know you are His friend, and gave him John 15:15. He turned to me and asked my name and said that was his favorite scripture. I got up and left, and didn't see him again until 1999.

On Dec. the 26th 1998, the Lord spoke to Bob, and said "I want you to move to Statesville, NC., and you are going to a conf. in Charlotte, and I have a Christmas present you haven't opened yet, and I am preparing a house for you in Statesville". This was spoken audibly to Bob at 6pm, and a friend of Bob's (Robby Knight) was fixing a meal for Bob and Viola at his house. When they arrived at the home the meal was just about ready, and Robby said to Bob,"you know Bob, I spent 3 months in Statesville, NC, and it was a really good three months". Bob said to Robby, " I never knew you stayed in Statesville, why are you telling me this", and he said "I don't know, but Statesville is really on my mind". Well Bob said " I understand why, the Lord just told me to move to Statesville". So Bob came to the New Year's Eve conf., and they took up a offering for Bob. It was a missionary offering, and Bob didn't know who it was for. They said they wanted to buy somebody a auto, and the Lord had spoke to Bob about a Oldsmobile (98), and told him that He was going to give him one. And I was wondering who the people at the conf. were talking about, and Rick Joyner said they were taking the offering up for Bob. This wasn't one of the big conferences, but the Tape of the month conf. There were about 1000 people there, and they took this offering up, and it was $75,000.

He went back to Fla, and called a real estate person to put his home on the market. He then went to a conf, and a man from Africa came, and gave Bob a word that he was going to be "joined with a joyner". Words just kept coming confirming what the Lord had spoken to Bob. So he got ready to move, but no one even was looking at his home.

Then Bob came to a conf. in April 1999 in NC, and one evening in the MFM room he was talking to some people about what the Lord had spoken to him, and Steve Lappin, who is a real estate person, was sitting listening. Bob was telling what kind of a home he would have when he moves to Statesville. He said it would be a brick home with a carport, and enough parking for a lot of cars, be one acre, and have a Jacuzzi, and be under $100,000, and Wanda Davis had a dream that the home would be a brown brick and have a pool. Steve laughed inside, but said to Bob he would love to help him find his home. He did a search and found a few homes that matched what Bob had said, and faxed them to Keith to give to Bob. Because Bob's home wasn't selling he never replied.

It was now the beginning of Sept 1999., and MorningStar was getting ready for their Boot Camp for the students coming in. As Bob was getting ready to come up to the boot camp, the Lord spoke to Bob, and said there is one sin that you haven't dealt with in your life, and he was thinking what that is, and He said resentment. "You have resented the betrayal and what people had done to you, and resentment is "sin". Bob didn't know that resentment was sin, and He said it was a part of unforgiveness and wanting the Lord to judge them. The Lord said for Bob to deal with the resentment, he had to forgive, and go and embrace those whom he had this toward and bless them. SO, Bob told the Lord he would. This took Bob two or three days to work through the repenting of this. Now remember it has been nine months and no one has come to see Bob's home for sale. Well, some people came by to see the home, and as they came up to the door, one of the men, said to Bob that there was a rattle snake on the ground, and Bob went a got a shovel and cut him in two, and buried him. He then thought, oh well, no need to bother with these people, because they won't want to buy this home after seeing this snake, but these people were from the area, and seeing a snake was a common thing. These people wanted to buy Bob's home.

Bob arrived at the airport in Charlotte for the Morningstar boot camp on Sept 6, 1999, and the Lord had told Bob he was to be moved in by Oct the 6th. He also told him that when he came up to the Charlotte area that he would be meeting three men, a Farmer, a Jewish Salesman from NY, and a Black man. Robin McMillan picked Bob and Viola up at the airport, and Bob told him that he needed to look for a home in Statesville on their way to the Boot Camp. Robin knew this realtor, Steve Lappin (who happened to be Jewish) and called him. He gave Robin a few homes that they could drive by and see it any of them interested Bob. The first home they drove by was a "brown brick" home with a carport, and a lot of parking had a "under contract" sign out front, but Bob really liked the way the outside looked, and he felt the Lord wanted him to have this home. Rick, also had some homes for Bob to look at, but in his heart Bob kept coming back to that "sold" brown brick home. He had Robin call Steve and ask if he could come the next morning and take Bob and Viola out to look at some homes. Steve came out the morning of the 7th of Sept, and picked up Bob and Viola. Then began to go and look at homes, but the ones they looked weren't for them. Bob asked Steve to see if we could get in to the home that said on the sign it was sold. Steve called the listing agent to see if they could get inside to see it, and would she take a back up offer on the home if we liked it. She said, "You aren't going to believe this, but the contract fell through last night". Well, Bob and Viola went to see the home, and of course it had a Jacuzzi in it, and had one acre, and as a bonus it had a olympic swimming pool. Oh, yes it was priced at $104,000. Bob wanted to pray on it that night. At the home he was staying at he was talking about what the Lord had told him about buying a 98 Olds, and a man (Brad McClendon) overheard him, and said I used to sell cars and I can help you. Bob called

Steve the next morning and told him he wanted to put in a offer at the tax value, which was $97,000. Steve submitted the offer not believing they would accept it , but they accepted it without making a counter offer, so Bob was able to buy the home under $100,000. So on the 8th of Sept. 1999, Bob bought a 98 olds and a home in Statesville, NC.

There was also something else that was going on. Remember the Lord spoke to Bob on Dec 26 about moving to Statesville. Well, when we were at the closing and talking to the sellers. They told us they were Christians, and Bob told them the story of how the Lord spoke to him, and said that they wish they would of known Bob, because that is when they put there home on the market.

Now this was the 8th of Sept, and Bob had to be out and up in NC by Oct the 6th. Bob had to finish the Boot camp, and after there that was a MFM retreat, and another conf. He didn't have time to think about anything, Bob had to go to Fla and get his home ready to close, and he came back up to Statesville to close on this home, so he went back to Fla to close on his home. On Sun night, Bob's friends helped him in renting a U-Haul, but it took till late Sun night to find one. They loaded up the truck that night. By 10:30pm they were loaded and packed and ready to go. Mon. morning of Oct 5th they started driving to NC, and Bob was wondering, "this is sure going quick and smooth, I have never seen it like this before. In NC Steve had put together a crew to help unload when Bob when they pulled into the home. They had gotten a refrigerator, and was waiting as the truck pulled in. So they set up their beds, and Bob and Viola slept in their own beds that night.

The next day the 6th of Oct , Steve went up to Bob's house to see how things were going, and they went out to eat at a local restaurant close by. When they were in line waiting to be served a young man kept looking at Bob, and then said "are you Bob Jones" "yep" he answered. He asked if Bob was visiting, and Bob said no, that he had just bought a home. Well, this man (Jeff Rowland, Pastor of Shiloh), started jumping up and down, saying he had been praying for Bob, and he knew it was the Lord for him to be hear, and he needs to meet this man right away. He put a call into someone, and told us not to leave until we meet this man. We finished eating and no-one had showed up. We got up to go outside, and we saw two men walking towards us. Bob had also told Steve that he needed to find a good doctor to hook up with also. When the men walked up to us, Bob said to the taller man, "I know you (for this was the farmer, and the Lord had told how Bob how many steps was on his porch and about a certain kind of business card in his wallet), and his name is Alan Smith (He is a farmer). Bob was talking to him, and in conversation said since you live here (oh by the way, he lives 2 miles from Bob's house). "do you know of a doctor in the area?". The man that came with Alan said "I am a doctor". Another thing the Lord had told Bob was he was going to stay on 77 hwy, and a angel came and gave him the 21st psalm. "he said to him that you are going to be on the 21st hwy and 77, and told he would live 2 miles off the 40 hwy. Well you know now that his home is 2 miles off hwy 40, and 3 miles from hwy21, and hwy21 crosses hwy77.

So the Lord put all this together by the 6th of Oct. 1999, just like he said he would. And Steve and Janis Lappin became very close friends with Bob and Viola. Bob would call Steve "his Jewish chauffeur" (I ended up driving for the Jones for the next 7 years), and he would call Janis "his upstairs maid" (Janis has this wonderful gift as a worshipper and intercessor).

I have so many wonderful memories of my time spent with Bob. I will forever be his friend.

ONE.
...BOB LOVED BASEBALL AND FOOTBALL
The Lord would speak to him through things going on around the world. Since it is the World Series time I am posting his experiences he shared with me of powerful prophetic experiences he had about Baseball.

The Royals had come from behind again for an 8th time in their

11 postseason games, securing their first World Series title since 1985 (click here for story).

It's been thirty years since Bob Jones' prophecy that the Kansas City Royals would be World Champs. In the spring of 1985 when Bob brought this wild and outrageous prophecy, the Royals were in the basement. People laughed and sneered at Bob calling him a false prophet, but God would prove him to be trusted and true. The Royals began to rise in the stats and go on to win the World Series against the St. Louis Cardinals.

In the fall of 2010 Bob was in a powerful trance where the Father took him to a baseball field and reminded him of past revelation. He also gave Bob understanding of the present condition of the Church and things to come. I want to share this powerful experience, which also includes both "Baseball Prophecies" from 1985 and 1995.

These prophecies were parables to the Church, establishing love, faith, godly wisdom, grace and justice. After thirty years (that represents the royal priesthood), Kansas City once again holds the title of winners of "The World Series". I believe the fact that the Royals made a comeback in the 12th inning scoring 5 runs says there is grace for the royal priesthood of Believers to establish new government. And they will be the "World Champions" as you will read in Bob's last prophecy about the Church being International. Intro was written by Bonnie Jones.

World Champions! A Prophetic Sign to the Church from Prophet Bob Jones,

Home Base

A couple of weeks ago, I was in a high level trance; one of the highest ones that I have known in recent years. The Lord came and took me to a field and it had been covered with snow for two years. We walked out on this field and He told me to uncover a place where He pointed. So I began to rake the snow away from the place that He said, and I realized it was a baseball plate. I didn't rake off all of the snow I just saw it was a baseball plate. And He said, "That's all I want you to see. This is home base and now

7

the sun will melt the snow off of the rest of it. You did all I want you to do right now. I just wanted to show you that this is home base."

I believe the Church is getting ready to come back to the bases. And home base is also the beginning and the end. It's where you start, and it's also where you win. I believe that we had a start, but I think we're coming into a year of winning.

Then He said, "Do you know what home base is?" And I'm thinking, No not really. He said, "I've given you revelation in the past where home base is. But mainly home base is going to be repentance and prayer. These things that I've shown you in the past, I can begin to bring it in step-by-step." He said, "This field had been snowed under for two years."

So I believe the Church is going through two years of really hard, dark times. It was like we didn't know where to go, and it was like a blanket of snow was on everything. I don't think this snow meant righteousness. I think it meant two years of trouble. These two years of trouble were coming to an end because it had accomplished some of the things it was meant to do.

Field of Dreams

He said, "This base is international!" So I'm not speaking about one church here; I'm speaking about the Church worldwide. And He reminded me that twice before I brought a prophecy about a baseball game. Also that it reminded me of a movie called, "Field of Dreams." So I think for two years we've been plowing things under in a time of not knowing what we were doing. But we were doing our best to obey what He was telling us to do just like the Field of Dreams. I believe that this "Field of Dreams" is getting ready to be revealed like it was in the movie. He told me to just repeat what you did twenty-five years ago.

Kansas City Royals – 1985

On May 21st of 1985, I brought a word in Kansas City about a baseball game, and it was about the Kansas City Royals. At that time the Kansas City Royals were then in the cellar. They hadn't won a game in quite a long while and nobody was paying much attention to them. My word was this, "The Kansas City Royals was going to come forth and was going to begin to win. They were going to be world champions in 1985." (Photo via flickr)

This is what I saw in the vision: I saw that it was the last half of the 9th inning and satan's team was in the field and the Lord's team was at bat, and the Lord's team had two outs. So the Lord sent in His first batter and this batter was Love. So satan pitched the ball and Love swung and it was a base hit. One on.

Love is the thing that's going to be the base. Love has got to be the basis of all things in Christianity. And I believe this is the year true Christians are going to be known for the love they have for one another. True servants of the Lord. They're going to be brought into a place of loving one another to where they have total control over their tongue, over their conversation, and how they express and present things. These three things: conversation, expression and presentation are going to be done in love. There's no defense the enemy has against love.

Instead of gossip, slander, and all of these wrong things, I think that when true disciples of the Lord speak, it will be something you want to listen to. Because if they haven't got something good to say about somebody, they won't say anything. But when they're saying something good about somebody you want to hear about it, because it's going to be the truth.

So, the first batter was Love. Well, faith worketh by love. Then the Lord sent His second batter out and His name was Faith. Faith pleases God and he can't fail. So, satan pitched the ball. Faith swung. Base hit. Two on!

So, I believe the Lord is calling us to a place of faith. Faith to me is three things. Humility to me is simply being obedient to the written Word of God, the logos, for it is the law book that shows us how to grow up. And if you grow up, your conversation is going to be right. I believe there's a work in humility that I could also call obedience, but you can also call it faith.

These three things I see as one: humility, obedience, and faith. You cannot study the Word without adding faith to it. If you obey it, then faith is going to automatically begin to move in you because you believe the logos. Then the living Words will start coming out of you. When it does, that faith can swing and it will be a base hit.

Then the Lord brought out His third batter. His name was Godly Wisdom. And satan pitched the ball, and Godly Wisdom looked over the ball and let it pass. Satan pitched the second ball; He looked it over and let it pass. Satan pitched a third ball; Godly Wisdom looked it over and also let it pass. Then satan pitched a fourth ball; Godly Wisdom looked it over and let it pass. You see, Godly Wisdom won't swing at what satan is throwing at him. (Photo via flickr)

Many times satan throws us things and our tongue can speak it, but Godly Wisdom won't allow it. Many times Godly Wisdom is in our ambitions and everything, because the enemy opens doors the Holy Spirit is not opening for us, and we enter those doors by not discerning whether the Lord wants us to or not. We should go to Him. When a door opens, we should go to find out who opens it, and you'll know real quick-like. Is it love? Is it faith? Well, if it's these things then it will be our witness to what the Holy Spirit's opening. But if it's our ambition, like money, then many times the enemy opens that door to distract us.

So Godly Wisdom looks them over and lets them all pass. Bases loaded! And the Lord is sending in a pinch hitter. Nobody's ever seen him before, and I don't think this generation has seen him. His name is Grace; great Grace. So satan winds up and pitches. It was a tremendous hit. And satan's hollering, "Don't worry about it. I've got beelzebub (another name for satan or demon) in center field and he's never let a fly get by." By the way, flies mean lies. And so the ball is going to center field and beelzebub is hollering, "I got it! I got it!" But it went right through his glove and banged him in the head, and down come beelzebub. Home run! Grand slam!

Why didn't Love, Faith, and Godly Wisdom get you through? They are only steps to prepare you for great Grace, and great Grace will get you home. The others will get you one base but great Grace will get you home!

I believe we are starting the Season of Love. And as we begin to love one another and be known throughout the world by the love we have for one another, we'll begin to see faith really rise up and get an answer to things. We'll begin to see the Body of Christ mature into Godly Wisdom to where we totally bridle our tongue so that when we speak, things happen. These are all a preparation for great Grace to get us home.

This was a parable of the Kansas City Royals when I brought it in 1985. They were in the cellar when I spoke this prophecy. I was pretty young in prophecy then and was really sweating it because it went all over town, and everybody said we'd know he's a false prophet because that's not going to happen.

Well, the Royals began to win immediately and they kept winning. They advanced to the World Series and the final game was played in Kansas City against the St. Louis Cardinals. After six games played they were tied with three games each. This was the final game of the series. And if I've ever seen a fix, Papa had a fix in on this game because the Cardinals were a powerful team, and everybody said Kansas City doesn't stand a chance because the Cardinals are a far better team. They had a far better coach and all the money was bet on the Cardinals.

So the game was played. It really got frustrating for the Cardinals because everything they did disintegrated, while everything the Royals did ended in home runs. It finally ended with the Royals 11 – Cardinals 0. I believe that number 11 is important because we are getting ready to start 2011.

TWO

Bob was always wanting to encourage the Church.

SHAKING - Winds and Storms, Floods, Fire, earthquakes, and mudslides. Don't let world events bother you. Look for Angels - be washed with the (water/Word), Fire, sanctification-supernatural fire. Shekinah - Be wrapped in a cocoon of Love. Stay in praise and peace. Stand in the gap- turn judgement into mercy. Pray for America - Bless the earth with rain from heaven.

Older Christians are the Joshua's of today. Bringing younger generation into the promised land. Their fruit will be our fruit

THREE

When you feel "wind" around you and you know it isn't a fan or AC. Angels are flying around you. You all are the only ones who can change anything on the earth. Invitation – Intimacy – to come into His presence. Step out in liberty and begin to shine. Stop limiting God – rejection is Sin. Resist distractions – let go of the past. Miracles are not optional – They're mandatory – activate your faith – be a doer – not just a hearer. Nothing happens till you open your mouth and speak. Don't live in the neutral – Business as usual is over.

We are filled with destiny- Get back to the basics – Power in the Blood. Take dominion over creation. Don't let your soul desire the credit. Don't limit God. Focus on the lover of your soul. Visions and dreams should be grounded by the logos Word.

FOUR

The Prophetic word spoken can apply today

I heard the Lord say that there has never been repentance made for the sin of Jonah! Immediately I checked the last chapter of Jonah and understood what God was saying. Jonah was exceedingly displeased and very angry because he knew that God was gracious and merciful and slow to anger. When the Ninevites repented, God revoked the sentence of evil against them and did not destroy them or their land.

Jonah's Sin Against God

God gave Jonah time to repent for his anger against Him, however he chose to sulk and wished in himself to die.

Jonah 4:9 And God said to Jonah, "Do you do well to be angry for the loss of the gourd?" And he said, "I do well to be angry, angry enough to die!" (Amplified)

As a Body of Believers we stood in agreement that we needed to make repentance for the sin of Jonah's anger against God. Jonah's pride prevented him from rejoicing at the victory of the message he delivered to Nineveh. He was probably the greatest evangelist that has ever lived.Over 120,000 people repented, turning that great city to righteousness.

A prophet's responsibility is obedience to God in delivering the word or message, but he is not allowed to judge it. Jonah should have had a heart of thanksgiving knowing that God's heart of love redeemed Nineveh for a greater purpose. A few days after we made repentance, the Lord awoke me in a profound way as I heard Him say, "Jonah, can you hear Me?" Then He gave me this awesome and heartfelt message about the Prophet Jonah. A message I believe all of us need to take to heart.

Jonah, My Prophet

"Jonah's tale is true. I abide yet this day in the hearts of My people because of Jonah's word.

"He was a strong man with a dreadful fear of Me, however he was overwhelmed by My word and mandate. Fear of man overtook him and he fled to Tarshish. I did not punish him," says God; "I loved him very much and therefore spared his life so he would complete his mandate in Me. "He did; he walked a crooked mile in fear and trembling.

Awestruck were the people of Nineveh at the sight of Jonah's perplexity. They readily repented and were full of My fear. However Jonah was disappointed in himself and My love for My people.

"Yes, repentance carries great rewards, and so I did not destroy Nineveh that day. She was very close to My heart for many years to follow.

"However, Jonah was still disappointed. I sent him away for a time and a season. His disappointment with Me was greater than his love for Me and My people. He became useless for My Kingdom and lived in self-pity the remainder of his years. "Did he obey Me? Yes, he did. Did he rebel? Yes, he did. Did he honor Me? Yes, he did until he became prideful and would not repent for his sin against Me.

"I cannot tolerate a haughty spirit," says God; "full of pride and self justification. I am merciful and triumph
over sin repeatedly.

"Now I say to you this day, pick up Jonah's mantle and go to Nineveh. This time repentance on your part will be
demanded first. My people will know My heart of love for them as you cry out mercy for them through repentance. My mercy triumphs over judgment.

"Where there has been little or no hope, faith will abound. Faith brings hope and hope deliverance and
deliverance brings new freedom in the spirit and the natural."

Jonah's Mantle

We are living in a time like that of Jonah's prophecy. The world is corrupted by sin and we are called to go
into the world and bring it to repentance. We are all called to pick up Jonah's mantle and go to the nations of
this earth. In all things we say and do we are supposed to shed God's light and love.

Jonah's name means dove, and dove means love. Our message to the world is repentance from sin through our
expression of love. It's time for the Jonahs to arise and go into the world with a message of God's heart of love
toward them. Love is the basis of all Christianity, for God is Love.

Repentance is the Key!

FIVE

Spending time with Bob was one of the most honored experiences of my walk with the Lord. Listening to him tell testimonies, revelations, and prophetic insights. I've come away with the understanding of who I am in the Lord. My life message is from Eph 4:14-16
Then we will no longer be infants, tossed back and forth by the waves, and blown here and there by every wind of teaching and

by the cunning and craftiness of men in their deceitful scheming. Instead, speaking the truth in love, we will in all things grow up into him who is the Head, that is, Christ. From Him, the whole body joined and held together by every supporting ligament, grows and builds itself up in love, as each part does its work.

John 17:17

Sanctify them by the TRUTH; your Word is TRUTH.

Revelation 19:10 "The testimony of Jesus is the Spirit of prophecy." Therefore, to acknowledge Jesus in scripture is to acknowledge prophecy.

1 Cor 14:1-5

Follow the way of love and eagerly desire spiritual gifts, especially the gift of prophecy. For anyone who speaks in a tongue does not speak to men but to God. Indeed, no one understands him; he utters mysteries with his spirit. "But everyone who prophesies speaks to men for their strengthening, encouragement, and comfort." He who speaks in a tongue edifies himself, but he who prophesies edifies the church. I would like every one of you to speak in tongues, but I would rather have you prophesy. He who prophesies is greater than one who speaks in tongues, unless he interprets, so that the church may be edified.

Prophesying is speaking in order to strengthen, encourage, and comfort others. It is not just speaking human encouragement; it is speaking divine encouragement. Prophecy is A hearing from God, and speaking what you hear in order to build, comfort, or encourage someone. Prophesy is to hear from God and speak to men. Just hearing isn't enough.

Bob would always say, One of the greatest ministries you can ever possess is the ministry of encouragement.

In a world without hope, people need the affirmation of God's love. Encouragement is the motivational force behind the ministry of Jesus and should also be the priority of all Christians.

SIX

Jesus can appear in a way not expected. One intercessor can break a plague. God desires our free will...Love Silence – His Presence is where time doesn't exist. Let not your heart be divided – Love not the world – Be still and know – Joshua lingered in God's Presence. Lay everything down on the alter. Sons of Levi are being purified. Christ sanctified Himself and emptied Himself of all His own desires. Become a living sacrifice. Bob loved Paul's statement in 1 Cor 2:2-5

For I resolved to know nothing while I was with you except Jesus Christ and him crucified. 3 I came to you in weakness and fear, and with much trembling. 4 My message and my preaching were not with wise and persuasive words, but with a demonstration of the Spirit's power, 5 so that your faith might not rest on men's wisdom, but on God's power.

That when he came to minister he was empty headed. We need to be empty headed so Jesus can fill us with His mind.

SEVEN

Blue stones – revelation gifts – original prophets in Wales and Scotland had blue stones and used them like Umin and Thummin - stones were faith contact. They brought conviction and truth. To hear the voice of God, you need to relax, rest in the Lord – REST – don't strain

Spiritual pornography – having thoughts on things of earth – worldliness, the pride of life, gossip, slander....

Disagreement - destroys faith

Negative faith – "I'm catching a cold" "I have an infection".. You are speaking it into existence

"I'm under the weather" Positive Faith – declare the Word and proclaim it...

God wants us to be a washerwoman – you can pray for others to be forgiven and washed.

Bob's heart was to bring us to his level

EIGHT

Once again Bob encouraged us to read Matthew 5,6,7 and Isaiah 55 every day for one month.

Patterns and formulas are the beginning of witchcraft. Patterns and formulas control others. We must operate in faith. Faith is showing up on time, empty-headed, ready to obey the Lord! Obedience is doing what the Holy Ghost puts in your head. You can't trust anything you cannot prove with the Word. Dreams need to point to the Word. If they do not, throw the dream away and do the Word! Obey the Word! The Word of God! Scriptures for further study include Matthew 15:6; Romans 10:8; Hebrews 6:5; 1st Peter 1:23; Revelation 19:13; Galatians 2:21.

By your words, you are justified or condemned. You should bless and curse – curse poverty, sickness, genetics.

You have to activate your faith to cause a prophecy to be fulfilled. Holiness – preferring others above yourself. Also Fruits of the Spirit. Trust is higher than faith.

Compassion – not critical or judgmental

Interpretation – Axe = book of Acts

Train – Glory – Train of his temple

Green = Teaching

Ask for the healing of the nations – physical, emotional, spiritual – also American Indian tribes

Keep asking for healing......Sin wounds the Lord

The order of the demonic or the order of demons are as follows:

#1. Mystic demons.

#2. Fallen Angels.

#3. Lust.

#4. Those who start religious wars.

#5. Animal spirits.

#6. Plagues or (blobs).

Ambition is an open door for demonic activity. Negative feelings reveal your heart. Anger in the beginning is flesh! The action of the tongue affects people eternally. Hurts will twist the soul.

The most miserable thing that can happen to a person or most miserable thing or place a person can be in is to be imprisoned to the sins and failures of the past. We are not entitled to pains and failures of the past.

We must begin now to separate the precious from the vile. Jeremiah 15:19. That which is precious must be put into our children...not anger...hatred...malice and other things that will twist their souls and damage and destroy their spirits.

NINE
I HOP
Many of us know about IHOP, but some of us only really know how it all began...Bob was living in Kansas City in 1983, when Mike Bickle was a young pastor in a church there. The first time Bob met Mike was March 7, 1983 (from Mikes own account). Bob told this story as if it was yesterday and how alive the word is when hearing it come from someone that experienced it and was walking in the anointing of a Prophet. Bob would often talk about Acts 2:19

I will show wonders in the heaven above and signs on the earth below, blood and fire and billows of smoke.

Bob said that the first thing he told Mike was God was going to raise up worldwide young adult prayer movement led by prophetic singers and musicians in Kansas City. Bob was told to wear a winter coat when he met with Mike...The temp that day was around 60, but he obeyed the Lord. Mike was very skeptical of the prophetic. Bob continued saying to prove he was who he said he was that we would see in the sky an unusual weather pattern. More specifically, he told Mike that on the first day of spring, snow would come, and he would be sitting around a table with him accepting his ministry. Well on March 21st Mike and Bob plus others were sitting around a table discussing the church's future and Bob was prophesying to Mike about his life, Mike realized the snow from that day was melting and Bob was prophesying. So sixteen years later IHOP was birthed.. Bob would go on to speak of things that would come. Sometimes it was to give the church a chance to pray against what the enemy wanted to do.

I remember before George Bush even declared that he was going to run for President Bob was sharing of an experience he had.... that he saw a burning bush and George Bush riding a bicycle on rough water. To Bob that meant he would become President and their would be trouble... Rough water in a vision meant to Bob "trouble". We know what happened on 9/11

TEN

Saints will die as a result of their own ambition! Bob saw a river of toxic human waste. Many Christians were lying in this river face up...floating...dead. It was a river of flesh and many ambitious people who wanted to be the head and not a servant were in this river. The spirit of rebellion will turn on those who do not repent from it!

Ezekiel 19:10 and John 15 are all about dwelling in the vine. Psalm 7:17 is all about "thanksgiving"! The Lord is looking for servants who have a heart of thanksgiving. God is raising up a people who can comfort people. We are coming out of the wilderness. Some in our midst that seem to be the weakest are the strongest and some who appear to be the strongest are the weakest.

Cedar means incorruptible flesh! God cohabits and lives through Scriptural Government. Isaiah 54:13 is for our children!

We must learn to release the enemy from his commission. For example, "I release you, spirit of infirmity, from your commission in the name of the Lord Jesus Christ.

Matthew 25:1-5 is a passage to be studied further. This passage speaks of the "virgin eagles".

Sowing is vital! We must sow! Do not eat your seed...sow it!!!

Giving and sowing is a must in order to build the Kingdom of God!

Betrayal is your greatest testing of compassion. The greater the violation...the betrayal...the greater the compassion!

The highest anointing brings the highest danger. Healings are a testimony of the Spirit of Prophecy which is the Spirit of Jesus.

ELEVEN

Josh 20:1-2

Then the LORD said to Joshua: 2 "Tell the Israelites to designate the cities of refuge, as I instructed you through Moses

Deut 12:5

But you are to seek the place the LORD your God will choose from among all your tribes to put his Name there for his dwelling. To that place you must go;

The Lord wants to put his name on cities for refuge.

When you dwell in the presence of the God you get healthier.

Isa 57, Ps113, Lk 11:11-12, Ps 138:6

Only one healing was initiated by Jesus; all others were asked for

Zech 4:7 authority inspired priesthood speaks by revelation.

Don't turn healing into ministry "This is my ministry"

Ez.47 River of blessing heals the land

The finger of God is on the trigger of our faith

Green = Teaching

Pray for healing between Arabs and Israel

Don't make decisions without seeking God first

Pray with (wait) the Lord, not to Him

Ps 125;3, Ps110:2, Isa 57:14 (we want the truth, not "a" truth), Ps 115, Isa 54:6-8

Outer court----Divine healing

Inner court-----Divine Health

Holy of Holies----Divine Life

Pray for financial blessing – whatever is your goal -DOUBLE IT A HUNDRED TIMES

Isaiah 11:5-Commitment. We get where we are going by commitment. Some religious people will not change and they will not get healed. Isaiah 11:11-The second time around! God holds His hand out for me...for us...for the second time around.

Our ceiling must be the floor for our youth!

If God gives you a vision, don't run with it until you get the provision! Get before the Lord and ask for the provision!

TWELVE
Overtaking the Thought Realm

Years ago Bob had a profound revelatory encounter in which he was shown the Mississippi River. In the experience, he was told of a significant application of this river in the strategy of Heaven. It was portraying the River of the Spirit with specific application to the Lord's plans for this nation.

He was given another experience in which he saw the Mississippi River again. Only this time he also observed four evil spirits that were represented by crocodiles. Although he was given a sharp sword to deal with these evil opposition's, he was instructed to harness their mouths and render them powerless. He put a bridle on their mouths and used their strength to move through the River at a great pace.

That in itself is a prophetic message to the church. Putting a bridle on our mouths can help nullify many of the schemes of the adversary set against Christians through the words we speak. Oftentimes we articulate the plans of the enemy when our revelation unknowingly comes from the "second" heaven rather than the third heaven where the plans of God are formulated.

The River was originally intended for fruitful spiritual purposes. Unfortunately, counterfeit spiritual authority hijacked the high purpose of Heaven for the River and the Lord is indicating His intent to take back possession of the River. According to Psalms

74:13-14,

You divided the sea by your strength; you broke the heads of the sea monsters in the waters. You crushed the heads of Leviathan; you gave him as food for the creatures of the wilderness. (Psalms 74:13-14)

There is a present work of the Spirit to sanctify the gifts and callings of Heaven so that they can be used for their ultimate destiny. Many of the false prophetic voices, the occult, and psychics to this generation actually possess genuine gifts that have not yet been sanctified. Once purified, then the gift becomes the food of the people. The same is true for many musical and creative gifts that are being utilized in the world rather than its highest purpose. The Lord is announcing His intent to redeem and reclaim those spiritual endowments.

Authority is being given to pull down the strongholds, arguments and every high thing that has set itself against the pure knowledge of God. This is the River that is to be purified. The Bible declares,

For the weapons of our warfare are not of the flesh, but divinely powerful for the destruction of fortresses. We are destroying speculations and every lofty thing raised up against the knowledge of God, and we are taking every thought captive to the obedience of Christ, and we are ready to punish all disobedience, whenever your obedience is complete. (2 Corinthians 10:4-6)

The weapons of our warfare empower us to refute unrighteous thoughts set against the knowledge of God. Every proud and lofty imagination that is harnessed against the true knowledge of God will be brought into captivity to the obedience of Christ. That is the sanctification process presently unfolding.

Unrighteous thoughts do not merely consist of sinful actions that we perceive as incorrect behavior. More fully, it includes any thought process we have that is not consistent with the nature and character of God and His word. These are the strongholds and dominions that attempt to taint our knowledge of God and the plan of heaven for this generation. The Lord's thoughts for us are lofty and powerful— we must come into agreement with that perspective.

THIRTEEN

The "I" stuff can really blow the anointing!
When "I" shows up...God goes!
Many will begin to pray and seek God, not just one person!
Picture of Copperhead snake is an unteachable Christian!
The Lord has now begun to reveal fruit...good and bad!
Papa is a single eye!
New Age is Hinduism with new clothes on it.
It is now time for the church to put its foot on the many curses that have been placed on it (curses on the church).
Prov 12:8 A man is praised according to his wisdom,
Wisdom joins you w/grace like a covenant of marriage
Wisdom we must seek her
Faith attitude – keep your healing
Speak a creative word Isa 48:6-7
Let Christ in me "Out"
You have to empty yourself
Religious spirit: Legalism, opinion, debate, criticism, judgment
I prayed for this person and they got healed..DON'T TAKE THE CREDIT
Depression – focus on self = false pride
Double rainbow – Covenant
Join yourself to what God's doing...Don't focus on self – idolatry
Worry is a SIN
Color Orange – tribe of Gad – speaks of companionship
Violating your conscience – lying, finances – Keeps you from hearing God

Heb 1:6 Angels have to come when there is worship
Real Prophecy is an invitation – Sin can cancel it – make it void
What happened in Toronto was Joy and Refreshing
What happened in Brownsville was repentance and commitment

FOURTEEN

Bob had many experiences with angels.

I remember Bob saying that many angels were unemployed because we either didn't believe in them or we never called upon them for assistance. He would also say that angels were assigned to us at birth and are with us throughout our life yet often times we don't see them. Angels escort us home to the Lord at the end of life's journey.

Psalms 91:11 says that God commands His angels to protect, defend and guard us in all our ways. I believe these are "watcher angels" that simply watch over us all of our life. And when we're about to encounter something dangerous this angel instructs other ones to prevent its occurrence. Can you remember a time when you just missed being struck by another vehicle or perhaps dodged a falling object? Do you remember how many people were detained for one reason or another on 9/11 that prevented their arrival at the twin towers? Angels on assignment will cause you to stay out of harm's way.

Bob depended on angels to assist him in ministry. Often times you would hear him say, "Feel the wind"? He was talking about angels. Hebrews 1:7 says, And concerning the angels He says, "Who makes His angels winds, and His ministering servants flames of fire (to do His bidding)." They are the wind and we are the fire and together we get the job done through obedience to the Father. Because Psalms 103:20 says, Bless the Lord, you His angels, you mighty ones who do His commandments, obeying the voice of His word! I always admired how Bob would wait to hear from the Holy Spirit what needed to be done in ministry. He didn't just jump the gun or shoot from the hip so to speak. He waited till he heard what was necessary for healing, a miracle or deliverance then he spoke. And the angels ministered with him.

He had two mighty angels named Emma and Grace that often traveled with him. He said their name is their job description; Emma means healing while Grace worked miracles. They made a mighty team. Yet many he called "Tinkerbells" because they are like small twinkling lights or fireflies. Often they show up as a confirmation to the truth of a prophetic word or that an assignment has been completed. Many times people have thought they "never" see angels but they see little twinkling lights. These are angels too but they have lesser assignments.

FIFTEEN

I KNOW THIS WILL STRETCH YOU

Heb 1:14 Are not all angels ministering spirits sent to serve those who will inherit salvation?

THE ANGEL BAG LADY

It was around December 2003 as the custom we were meeting at Bob's home every Wed. to spend time and see what the Lord is doing. There were about 8 of us there with Bob. Viola (Bob's wife) would always sit and listen not ever saying much. Bob was like a fountain pouring out revelation and wisdom to us. Bob like he did (his eyes lit up) and said "you're the one I saw in my dream". He said Ken and Brenda stand up please. He put his hands on both of their shoulders and says I bless you God bless you, I bless you in the name of Jesus Christ. Then I stood up and said you're not getting out of here without blessing me too! He laughed and put his hands on me too. There was a brother from Asheville (David) there and had been looking to open a place in the mountains near Asheville to bring in folks to disciple. He was telling us that he needs $600,000 dollars to seal the deal on the land he wanted to purchase. He said I am taking this word for me too. Bob was known to have some powerful dreams and trances that changed lives and circumstances in people's lives.

Well he began to tell us of this dream that caused all of this stuff happening. He began saying he was sitting in his chair and all of a sudden an old lady walked up to him with a big bag. She asked him who do you want me to take this money too, and opened the bag and he saw a lot of money. Bob said he wanted it to go to those that want to build the Kingdom. He described this woman (who we all knew was a Angel) as a old Italian lady. He said he remembered that in the early days of the 1900's the mob used little old ladies to bring the money to places in big shopping bags. One thing I learned when you hear a word from the Lord to a person you can also take it for yourself. We all left that day thinking about what we now called this Angel "The Angel Bag Lady". You might say this is ridiculous, well let me tell you what happened.

Because of the holiday's we didn't meet again until around the second week of Jan. We all got to Bob's house around 11am (the time with him would always end with going to lunch around 1:00). David was there and you could see that he was busting with something going on. Bob in only the way he could say "ok tell us what happened" (Without hesitation Bob believed what the Lord had shown him about the Angel Bag Lady was true and would happen) David began by telling us that he was looking for investors to support his project, when he came upon this woman (who looked Italian) and when he finished telling her about his project, she said I would love to help, and she had are you ready!!!! $600,000 cash she wanted to invest. Well the living room lit up and you could feel the Faith of the Lord pouring over us. I knew this was for me also.

I was doing real estate as you saw in that I helped Bob purchase his first home here in NC. By the end of Jan I had a little over 1 million in sales. Wow!! This was crazy...I told Bob and he just chuckled and said what did I expect. I thought about that. I always would listen to what Bob would say, because in just talking to you revelation would come sometimes. "What did I expect". Yes Lord I expect the Angel Bag Lady to come to me and help me. I told Janis and she was amused, but didn't have the same faith that I had mainly because she wasn't sitting in Bob's living room and experienced the revelation pouring over us. Well Feb was coming to an end and I was at about $800,000 in sales, and on the last day of the month I had a $250,000 sale. Now Janis was getting excited. She would walk around the house and of course thank the Lord, but bust out and say "Thank you Angel Bag Lady". If someone was listing to us they would think we were crazy. Well the months went on and by the end of every month I produced over 1 million in sales every month. 2004 ended being the best year in real estate that I ever had. I was the top producer in Charlotte for a Lake Norman community. I won a trip to Atlantis for 8 nights all expenses paid with Janis. I won a lease on a Mercedes that I converted to cash and bought a Pre-Owned Mercedes.

Ken and Brenda sold custom made jewelry in Asheville. They came back with a testimony of how the Angel Bag Lady also helped them. They sold over $50,000 in one weekend. It was all of their merchandise, so that meant they were able to keep all the money....

Over the years when we were in the valley (of decision) we would cry out to the Lord, and (we believe) He would send His Angel Bag Lady to help us.

It was 2007, and real estate had fallen through to the bottom. This was the only source of income Janis and I had. We went two years without a paycheck, but the Lord saw us through. We almost lost our home, but the Lord saw us through.

From 2008 to 2012 was hard years learning to trust the Lord, and believe He would come through for us. 2012 to 2016 was learning to climb the mountain out of the valley, but it was a decision to take the steps to climb that has brought us to today. We believe over the years the Lord would send the Angel Bag Lady when we needed her.

SIXTEEN

Like many of Bob's prophetic experiences, it would be like an allegorical encounter continuing to convey important principles essential for our development and training for Spiritual releases from Heaven. Prophetic symbolism is utilized to communicate prominent spiritual truths essential to enter into a covenant relationship with the Lord for spiritual service or ministry. Listening to Bob speak this way would cause you to dig deep to ask the Lord how does this apply to me. Listening to Bob share about his experience where in a vision he was taken to a temple in which a highest form of praise was taking place. In the midst of this high level praise, an old man walked into the service in a very unkempt manner. In fact, his hair was long and stringy covering not only His head but also his face. He had somewhat stooped shoulders and acted frail and confused by external demeanor. He looked like a very old wilderness sage. Most who saw this seemingly ancient looking man simply assumed he was a confused elderly man and gave him little attention. As he moved through the crowd in this physical condition, he inquired of the people asking, "Do you know me? Do you know me?" As He did so, most did not even acknowledge his presence nor did they recognize his voice. However, immediately upon hearing this old man's voice Bob instantly recognized that it was the Lord, although the outward appearance was strange and unique. He identified Him by

His voice.

After that, He appeared in a different form to two of them while they were walking along on their way to the country. (Mark 16:12)

In the vision, He was not easily recognizable externally, yet those who were intimately acquainted with Him could straightaway discern His voice.

Bob was then asked, do you know Me more intimately than your own wife? The Lord is requiring in this hour an even more affectionate relationship with us than we have with our spouse. Even among a crowd of people or in a completely dark circumstance, we can clearly and easily recognize the voice of our spouse. We are being challenged in this hour to be still more intimately acquainted with the Lord than our own spouse and know more distinctly His Voice than any other. In this manner, no matter the form in which He comes, we can recognize Him because His Voice designates His presence.

My sheep hear My voice, and I know (become intimately acquainted with) them, and they follow Me; and I give eternal life to them, and they will never perish; and no one will snatch them out of My hand. (John 10:27-28)

When Bob recognized the Voice of the One with whom he was speaking, he knew intuitively it was the Lord Himself. Immediately, he found himself expressing with great fervency all of the divine titles that were quickened to his spirit. You are the Lion of Judah, the Lord of Lords, the anointed Son, Christ– Son of the Living God. You are the one who is and who was and who is to come, the Branch and Captain of the Hosts. These were only a few of the many divine attributes and titles that emanated from his spirit upon acknowledging this old man was literally the Lord Himself in another form.

After hearing the expression of His divine titles, the Lord acknowledged that He is indeed all of those things and if a person can recognize His Voice in such a manner, he then qualifies to be given the opportunity to be SEALED for divine service. After saying this, the Lord approached with both of His hands and placed them under Bob's left shoulder in the gesture of a covenant. He then said, If you know Me, and you know Me intimately along with My love and fulfill the law through love, then I will seal you for service in a covenant relationship.

Love does no wrong to a neighbor; therefore love is the fulfillment of the law. (Romans 13:10)

Bob was then commissioned to do likewise to others willing to make this commitment and entreat them to readily recognize His Voice so they too can be sealed for service in the endeavors about to be released in the earth. The scriptures declare that He who establishes us in Christ and anoints us is God is the One who also seals us and gives the Spirit in our hearts as a pledge or covenant. (2 Corinthians 1:21-22)

Nevertheless, the firm foundation of God stands, having this seal, "The Lord knows those who are His," and, "Everyone who names the name of the Lord is to abstain from wickedness." (2 Timothy 2:19)

Finally in the vision, upon closer observation, Bob could see through the white hair that rested over the Lord's face and was able to distinguish that He was coming with the facial features of a Lion. He will represent Himself through this company of sealed servants/friends as the Lion of the Tribe of Judah and impart a warlike Spirit to those of His people willing to enter into covenant relationship with Him. His face resembled the features of a lion, yet His eyes were like flaming fires.

Bob felt that the Lord was saying to the church, Those who are sealed will begin to be groomed as warring commanders like the tribe of Gad. Some will be leaders of hundreds and others leaders of thousands. This distinguished group will be those who cross over during times of trouble. The Gaddites crossed the Jordan during flood season suggesting a season of trouble. This company will be determined warriors well equipped who will not retreat in battle; Nor will they be denied victory and will put to flight all that stands between them and the divine purposes for which they are commissioned. Although it will be during seasons of distress in the world, these commissioned warriors will march tirelessly with resolute determination, resting assuredly in their covenant relationship with the Lord, and TRUST IN THE LORD.

These were from the sons of Gad, captains of the army; the least was over a hundred, and the greatest was over a thousand. These are the ones who crossed the Jordan in the first month, when it had overflowed all its banks; and they put to flight all those in the valleys, to the east and to the west. (1 Chronicles 12:14-15)

SEVENTEEN

Amos 9:13 Harvest coming in

Isa 28:17 Ice(winter-fasting) sweeps away lies – Biggest lie "God doesn't love me" " I am not worthy" None of us are, it is the grace of God

The Lord wants to set us free from guilt. Hopelessness is trying to get a hold of people

Speak the truth – light comes forth

God has given awesome authority to the Church

Money shouldn't be a pressure not to do what God wants

Quit buying the lie.

Jer 5:1 it can only take one person to change things

Give all insecurity, envy, jealousy, ambition, timidity to God

Don't hold on to these things – Focus on Jesus – Not yourself

You can move in all nine gifts.

Stop limiting God in your life.

Your spirit –"I want to be heard-I want (my) anointing to be seen"

Defilement of conscience – I want a (certain) car; I WANT.....(Lust of eyes, flesh)

Timidity – false pride

Plagues will not come near you

Vision of ship = leadership, Ocean=humanity, flowers=flesh, ashes=repentance,

Floods=troubles, hospital=wounded

Don't talk about what the enemy does – TALK ABOUT WHAT JESUS DOES

Confidential sin – don't share it with others

Five levels of demonic order:

1. Fallen angels 2. Lust spirit 3. Mystic -fortune tellers 4. Animal sprits 5. Plagues

Grumbling is evil

After deliverance – whatever was delivered (spirit of anger, fear etc) will try to attack you –

Pray a hedge around you. If you have female problems stop praying for others for a season.

Resist humanistic, soulish compassion

You must be positive- don't produce negative energy

Commissioning – anointing

Tabernacle of David fell because of a breach – fill the breach in with praise, power, prophecy

Trust = Obedient ....example

Jesus is at Niagra falls and there is a line across from one side to the other.

Jesus is going to push a wheelbarrow across. Do you Trust He will. Then get in and you are Obedient.

Your genetics change when you commune with God.

EIGHTEEN

Bob told us about his revelation of the
OX, EAGLE, LION AND MAN

In a vision Bob was told to push a button. In doing so a voice spoke declaring, "IT HAS BEGUN". Through this the Lord is saying that he has begun His "showing" and His "shining". He is beginning the showing of His justice and the shining of His glory in this world. It is as though the Lord is being awakened from a slumber.

Bob said the Holy Spirit is announcing that He is now going to release the revelation of His Word bringing people back into an intimate relationship with Him. This intimate relationship can be achieved through the four gospels. The four gospels outline relationship with the Lord. Our Elder Brother is going to reveal Himself through the four symbols of revelation. The symbol of the ox, the eagle, the lion, and the man. Bob said he was then shown a large cedar log that was flat on each end. On one end of the log he saw the image of an ox. The ox is utilized in the plowing of fallow ground preparing the soil for sowing and reaping. During the time of plowing, however, evidence of progress cannot be easily seen by the workers. All that is visible is the plowed ground and the working of the ox without the evidence of fruit.

The season of the ox sees nothing but the old dead harvest and the monotony of plowing. This type ministry is necessary for the preparation of the following stage. However, with this preparation and awakening comes the mess that an ox will often create. The ministry of the ox can best be described through the book of Matthew; specifically, the teachings of the Lord known as the "Be Attitudes". Blessed are the poor in Spirit for they do not think more highly of themselves than they ought. This attribute is significant in defining the ox ministry. While the ox ministry is active, it creates a hunger and a thirst within the people. The Scriptures also declare "Blessed are they that hunger and thirst for they shall be filled".

Bob said the vision continued, the cedar log with the emblems imprinted upon it began turning counterclockwise. The next symbol that Bob saw was that of an eagle. This is the season of the Spirit in which we are now merging. The Lord indicated that this symbol was represented in the book of Mark. The special emphasis placed upon this book is the 16th chapter of Mark representing the ministry of the eagle.

The ministry of the eagle is necessary to impart vision for the discipleship of nations; men and women filled with the Holy Spirit going into all the earth preaching the gospel, casting out demons, healing the sick, and dealing with demonic opposition without fear.

The cedar log continued to turn and Bob said he saw that the next symbol was that of a lion represented by the book of Luke. Luke 10:19 declares "behold, I give you the authority to trample upon serpents and scorpions, and over all the power of the enemy, and nothing by any means shall hurt you."

The Lord is saying that it is His good pleasure to give us the kingdom. The lion is a symbol of ultimate kingly authority; the authority to exercise His dominion over all the power of the enemy. If we by the finger of God cast out demons then the kingdom of Heaven is among us.

The next symbol that Bob saw as the cedar log continued to turn counterclockwise was that of MAN. This symbol was represented by the book of John. John was declared to be the FRIEND OF GOD. This representation displays the Lord's desire for friendship and an intimate relationship with His people as defined by John 15, 16 and 17. These are the type friends with whom the Lord can share His secrets, those who will be completely trustworthy with the mysteries and power of God.

The Lord is the Vine and we are His branches. It is now time for us to begin to bear fruit even as the early apostolic church bore fruit for eternal purposes. It is by becoming one with the Father that we share in His attributes and His potentials.

NINETEEN

Handmaiden – hand picked by the father – It's a call- you will be summoned – Holiness unto the Lord

Sonbirds from heaven can come and sit on your shoulder and give spontaneous songs that rhyme –take the risk – don't prepare beforehand. Come empty headed.

Intercession can lessen any judgment. This was around 2003 Bob spoke of Millennial power. Power of the world to come... 7th day...maybe a thousand years or not

God will show favor to Zion now..From the 2000 on we will see 1 billion youth come to the Lord. They will be the Dread champions – pray for power for others.

Hospital wings will be cleared out! Bob talked about 9/11. He said Terrorism =911 – Psalm 91:1

He who dwells in the shelter of the most High will abide in the shadow of the Almighty! OUR SAFETY.

Aging is a curse of the fall. You are a new creature – act like it and speak to your soul "newness of life".

The job of intercession is to open the prison doors and set the captives free. Be willing to serve the least. John 16:13 "Holy Spirit - what have you heard that you want to tell me" "But when He, the Spirit of truth, comes, He will guide you into all the truth; for He will not speak on His own initiative, but whatever He hears, He will speak; and He will disclose to you what is to come".

Fill your home with praise and worship music.

Pity = agreeing with their circumstances. Don't receive any sickness – reject everything that comes against the Word of God. Keep pushing it back. "devil – you can't have anything of mine!"

Break the spirit of poverty over NC.

Look over the book of Col, Rom 13:10

Job 36:29 and 37:5

Shoulder offering – covenant

Quit having a reason to repent

Obedience(faithfulness, humility) is higher than repentance

Putting a bridle on our mouths can help nullify many of the schemes of the adversary set against Christians through words we speak. Oftentimes we articulate the plans of the enemy when our revelation unknowingly comes from the "second" heaven rather than the third heaven where the plans of God are formulated.

For the weapons of our warfare are not of the flesh, but divinely powerful for the destruction of fortresses. We are destroying speculations and every lofty thing raised up against the knowledge of God, and we are taking every thought captive to the obedience of Christ, and we are ready to punish all disobedience, whenever your obedience is complete. (2 Corinthians 10:4-6)

The weapons of our warfare empower us to refute unrighteous thoughts set against the knowledge of God. Every proud and lofty imagination that is harnessed against the true knowledge of God will be brought into captivity to the obedience of Christ. That is the sanctification process presently unfolding.

Unrighteous thoughts do not merely consist of sinful actions that we perceive as incorrect behavior. More fully, it includes any thought process we have that is not consistent with the nature and character of God and His word. These are the strongholds and dominions that attempt to taint our knowledge of God and the plan of heaven for this generation. The Lord's thoughts for us are lofty and powerful— we must come into agreement with that perspective.

TWENTY

Macaroni and Cheese

When Bob told us about this word he got it began an understanding for me about how the Word of Knowledge works. Bob was at a church that he was verily new too. He was sitting and enjoying the worship when the Lord spoke to him the words "Macaroni and Cheese". Bob pondered this and put this thought aside, but it kept coming back to him. So feeling like a fool he blurted out the words "Macaroni and Cheese". Everyone in the church turned and looked at him as if he was crazy, and some even laughed. Bob felt rejected and left that church not to go back again. The story about what Bob did began to spread and a woman that was praying for her son to come to know the Lord heard the story, was greatly moved. No one knew about what her son did for a living. He drove a delivery truck and on the side of the truck were the words "Macaroni and Cheese". She knew that the Lord heard her prayers. It was at a later date that she was at a conference that Bob was also there. She went up to him and shared how that word impacted her with faith to believe. Bob had gone for a long time wondering how God could give him such a crazy word that people would laugh at him, but now he understood it isn't what the word is, but the impact it can have in someone's life no matter how funny, or crazy it might seem. Over the years the Lord would give Bob many visions, trances, and experiences that didn't make sense till he spoke them and asked for understanding. Hearing this testimony from Bob gave me the confidence to step out in faith even when I might think this is crazy. This is were I call faith "RISK".

Just a few of examples that happened to me: When praying for people I would get a word or picture that didn't make sense to me, but I shared anyway. I was with two other people on a Sunday after the service and people were coming up to ask for prophetic words. They would sit in front of the three of us, and we would ask the Lord for His heart for them. According to 1 Cor 14:3 we would speak. This would last for about 8 to 10 minutes. In walked this brother and sat down in front of us. I prayed and then listened, and I heard the words "Babbling idiot for Jesus". I sat there and reasoned with myself that this is crazy and I can't say that. The pressure mounted on my spirit to say these words, and I said to myself ok, I will be a fool for Christ. I looked at him and said, "I hear the Lord calling you a Babbling idiot for Jesus". He literally fell out of his chair laughing. We looked at each other and knew something happened, but not knowing what all this meant. He got up and left and didn't say anything to us. The background on this brother was that he was a Baptist pastor who had gotten filled with the spirit and his friend asked him to come to our meeting. He had never been prophesied over till this time. But at his church, his friends would say to him all the time "Hey Carroll you're a Babbling idiot for Jesus". This began what would become a lasting friendship with him and me for many years until he went home to be with the Lord.

Another time we were in the midst of having a "School of the Spirit" at this Baptist church on Monday nights seeing these hungry people come and get filled with the spirit. On this Monday night after the service, we would have prayer and people would come up for prayer. This woman came up to me, and as I was getting ready to pray, she said: "you can tell me what is happening in my life". I stepped back and looked at her and this word popped out of my mouth. "it isn't and wasn't your fault". She crumpled on the floor crying uncontrollably. We came to find out that a couple of months before she was in an accident and her child was sitting next to her and was killed. She had been blaming herself all this time, and in that moment God healed her heart.

You know how sometimes you hear a word or have a thought and it is a cliché. Well, people were coming up to us for prophetic words after church, and this pregnant woman walks in and sits in front of us. We started to pray and began to hear the song "He has the whole world in His hands". I said to myself that isn't what I am going to say, of course, he does and she has heard that maybe a hundred of times. The spirit kept prompting me to say this, I said to her "the Lord wants you to know He has the whole world in his hands and it will be ok". She began to cry and the Iraq war had just started. Her husband was in the army and had left that week. This seemingly cliché word had given her much comfort.

1 Cor 14:3 But everyone who prophesies speaks to men for their strengthening, encouragement, and comfort.

You can't go wrong when your motivation is to do this.

TWENTYONE

Bob had a powerful vision in 2001, which I know can relate to today:

In this experience, Bob was taken to a temple in which highest form of praise was taking place. In the midst of this high level praise, an old man walked into the service in a very unkempt manner. In fact, his hair was long and stringy covering not only His head but also his face. He had somewhat stooped shoulders and acted frail and confused by external demeanor. He looked like a very old wilderness sage. Most who saw this seemingly ancient looking man simply assumed he was a confused elderly man and gave him little attention. As he moved through the crowd in this physical condition, he inquired of the people asking, "Do you know me? Do you know me?" As He did so, most did not even acknowledge his presence nor did they recognize his voice. However, immediately upon hearing this old man=s voice Bob instantly recognized that it was the Lord, although the outward appearance was strange and unique. He identified Him by His voice. The very One the congregation was in the temple worshiping moved in among the people, yet in a different form.

After that, He appeared in a different form to two of them while they were walking along on their way to the country. (Mark 16:12)

In the vision, He was not easily recognizable externally, yet those who were intimately acquainted with Him could straightaway discern His voice.

Bob was then asked, do you know Me more intimately than your own wife? The Lord is requiring in this hour an even more affectionate relationship with us than we have with our spouse. Even among a crowd of people or in a completely dark circumstance, we can clearly and easily recognize the voice of our spouse. We are being challenged in this hour to be still more intimately acquainted with the Lord than our own spouse and know more distinctly His Voice than any other. In this manner, no matter the form in which He comes, we can recognize Him because His Voice designates His presence.

My sheep hear My voice, and I know (become intimately acquainted with) them, and they follow Me; and I give eternal life to them, and they will never perish; and no one will snatch them out of My hand. (John 10:27-28)

When Bob recognized the Voice of the One with whom he was speaking, he knew intuitively it was the Lord Himself. Immediately, he found himself expressing with great fervency all of the divine titles that were quickened to his spirit. You are the Lion of Judah, the Lord of Lords, the anointed Son, Christ– Son of the Living God. You are the one who is and who was and who is to come, the Branch and Captain of the Hosts. These were only a few of the many divine attributes and titles that emanated from his spirit upon acknowledging this old man was literally the Lord Himself in another form.

When the Lord is fully manifested, He brings with Him all of His redemptive attributes. All that the Father is was expressed in the Person of Jesus Christ. Through the Spirit, all that the Lord Jesus is will be depicted through the Bride, the Body of Christ. This will give expression to the full array of redemptive qualities resident in the Lord and purchased for man through the cross.

After hearing the expression of His divine titles, the Lord acknowledged that He is indeed all of those things and if a person can recognize His Voice in such a manner, he then qualifies to be given the opportunity to be sealed for divine service. After saying this, the Lord approached with both of His hands and placed them under Bob's left shoulder in the gesture of a covenant. He then said, If you know Me, and you know Me intimately along with My love and fulfill the law through love, then I will seal you for service in a covenant relationship.

Love does no wrong to a neighbor; therefore love is the fulfillment of the law. (Romans 13:10)

Bob was then commissioned to do likewise to others willing to make this commitment and entreat them to readily recognize His Voice so they too can be sealed for service in the endeavors about to be released in the earth. The scriptures declare that He who establishes us in Christ and anoints us is God is the One who also seals us and gives the Spirit in our hearts as a pledge or covenant. (2 Corinthians 1:21-22)

Nevertheless, the firm foundation of God stands, having this seal, "The Lord knows those who are His," and, "Everyone who names the name of the Lord is to abstain from wickedness." (2 Timothy 2:19)

With the commission to go to the church with the purpose of sealing others for service, the Lord gave this additional admonition. He stressed the importance of these purposes and acknowledged this was no small matter. The days in which we are entering are of utmost importance as it relates to kingdom purposes. The events in the earth are about to become so significant and even traumatic, that this relationship with the Lord is of paramount importance if we are to survive and even thrive. We cannot enter into covenant relationship with the Lord carelessly nor presumptuously. To make a vow or promise to the Lord is a serious matter requiring resolute determination to fulfill our spiritual obligations. Our constant cry should be for the grace and spiritual provision to faithfully fulfill our promises to the Lord in this covenant commitment.

When you make a vow to God, do not be late in paying it; for He takes no delight in fools. Pay what you vow! It is better that you should not vow than that you should vow and not pay. (Ecclesiastes 5:4-5)

Along with this commission, there will be a strong impartation of intercessory prayer to those sealed in this manner.

Finally in the vision, upon closer observation, Bob could see through the white hair that rested over the Lord's face and was able to distinguish that He was coming with the facial features of a Lion. He will represent Himself through this company of sealed servants/friends as the Lion of the Tribe of Judah and impart a warlike Spirit to those of His people willing to enter into covenant relationship with Him. His face resembled the features of a lion, yet His eyes were like flaming fires.

Those who are sealed will begin to be groomed as warring commanders like the tribe of Gad. Some will be leaders of hundreds and others leaders of thousands. This distinguished group will be those who cross over during times of trouble. The Gaddites crossed the Jordan during flood season suggesting a season of trouble. This company will be determined warriors well equipped who will not retreat in battle; Nor will they be denied victory and will put to flight all that stands between them and the divine purposes for which they are commissioned. Although it will be during seasons of distress in the world, these commissioned warriors will march tirelessly with resolute determination, resting assuredly in their covenant relationship with the Lord.

These were from the sons of Gad, captains of the army; the least was over a hundred, and the greatest was over a thousand. These are the ones who crossed the Jordan in the first month when it had overflowed all its banks; and they put to flight all those in the valleys, to the east and to the west. (1 Chronicles 12:14-15)

Bob said that there will be a release of the Spirit for leadership to begin to seal for service those who are willing to make this commitment. With it will come significant advances in an intimate relationship with the Lord and notable increases in power. They will be as a spiritual troop of Gadites equipped and prepared for the divine purposes about to be released. However, the warning continues to echo that it is no small thing to enter into a covenant relationship with the Lord if the intent is not there to wholeheartedly fulfill it.

integrity and loyalty

It takes holiness to get through the 2nd heaven – faith

Paul saw a heavenly vision

Armor of light Eph 5:8-14 For you were once darkness, but now you are light in the Lord. Live as children of light 9(for the fruit of the light consists in all goodness, righteousness, and truth) 10 and find out what pleases the Lord. 11 Have nothing to do with the fruitless deeds of darkness, but rather expose them. 12 For it is shameful even to mention what the disobedient do in secret. 13 But everything exposed by the light becomes visible, 14 for it is light that makes everything visible.

1 Peter 2:9 But you are a chosen people, a royal priesthood, a holy nation, a people belonging to God, that you may declare the praises of him who called you out of darkness into his wonderful light.

What God appoints what He anoints

Col 1:13 – integrity, holiness, faith

See vision by faith Isa 48:6 "You have heard; look at all this. And you, will you not declare it? I proclaim to you new things from this time, Even hidden things which you have not known.

Invitation for a visitation

TWENTY TWO
THE BEGINNING OF BOB'S MESSAGE TO THE BODY OF CHRIST

"It was 1975 August the 8th a demon appeared to me, and said "If you ever share prophecy again I will kill you." I told him, "I don't belong to you anymore, I belong to the Lord...I stood before the Lord in death because I brought some prophesies the devil didn't like. ""Like there would be some homosexual disease you couldn't cure. Abortion was going to be formed in such horrible ways it made people sick when I brought them, so they didn't welcome me back in their churches. And I bought words like there will be chemicals, cheap chemicals they mix together and there would be a horrible, soul killing drug: Meth labs.. I had been so sick. I kept getting worse in so much pain and blood was shooting out of my mouth like a geyser. And I went to the Lord because of these prophesies. And I died in great pain.

And I went into a tunnel and there was a man that stood beside me. He was all white. I have never seen His face. He is the Parakleet, the Holy Spirit.

I walked out of a tunnel and a light come on me, that I wish I could tell you how good it felt. Of all the good existence that you have ever lived, if you put them in one sentence, they would actually be nothing compared to how well I felt. I felt so secure, so loved. I was wrapped up in the anointing of God, it was like white light. I never felt so loved. I asked the Lord what is this? He said it's the love of God. I said, the love of God is white? He said no, the glory of

God is white. What is this? It's the glory and love of God in John 17.

I have given to them the glory and honor which You have given Me, that they may be one [even] as We are one: I in them and You in Me, in order that they may become one and perfectly united, that the world may know and [definitely] recognize that You sent Me and that You have loved them [even] as You have loved Me. Father, I desire that they also whom You have entrusted to Me [as Your gift to Me] may be with Me where I am, so that they may see My glory, which You have given Me [Your love gift to Me]; for You loved Me before the foundation of the world.

As I drew close to Him I saw the great and the small. I saw on one side, people going to hell. And they were great number. On my side there were few. And when they come before Him. He would only ask you one question when you stand before Him. Did you learn to love? You are born in a fallen condition. If you learn to love, then you are going to do all the other things you are supposed to do. {I John chapters 3,4 & 5}

So He said, the enemy killed you before your time, I want you to go back. I told Him I'm not doing any good, nobody is listening to me. He said, you are a liar because you spoke My Words and My Words will happen. I said it was pretty painful back there and He said, you are sort of a coward too. But when you were a Baptist, you had a love for souls. If you can look at those that's going another place, and want to come in, I will bring you in. But if you go back, you will see the beginning of Me bringing a billion youth unto Myself. The greatest harvest of all times!"

TWENTY THREE
God's invitation – "Come and visit me"!
3 Intercessors can change the world – America " Let your Kingdom come" Open up the ancient wells. Pray with God – Ask Him what to pray. Listen and pray His heart.
Israel is the apple of God's eye!
Outer court is healing; inner court is divine health

Miracles come from creative imagination
Take communion – it is the Tree of Life
Get a vision to share with youth
Mix your old wine with their new wine
What is your part of the harvest?
God says "Slaves work for me – Friends work with me"
You are seated in heavenly places on the throne with Christ NOW
Speak blessings to your body. You can change your DNA
You are a new creation.
Attack against hope, family – death

"Bob's vision" people bringing fruit to the feet of the Lord. Happy birthday Jesus
large carton of oranges – Kiss the Son, peaches, apples, Bob had a small basket of big grapes.
Laid them at His feet and Jesus said "thankyou"
The only thing you can bring me is "fruit"
Every time you stand against the enemy you are bringing me fruit
1. Orange – Kiss the Son – Sweet companionship of the Lord, He is our greatest pleasure Ps25:14
2. Peach – Joy – sense of well being – The Lord is pleased with you – Iam pleasing the Lord "the joy of the Lord is my strength"
3. Apple – Peace – Stay in peace – you are being healthy – freedom from disturbing thoughts – we are no longer slaves to thoughts and emotions.
4. Pear – Patience – long life – enduring life without complaining – 150 year old children, childrens, childrens bearing fruit.
5. Tomato – Kindness – big hearted and very generous, time, money – with your life
6. Strawberry – goodness – low – humble – virtue – healing – sweet, bear fruit in the Son – they are small in their own eyes, but very sweet
7. Grapes – Faithfulness – loyal – a lot of our testing lately is saying "NO" to our options
8. Banana – Gentle, it builds the heart
9. Grapefruit – Self control – sweet(loyal)-sour(keep putting to

death the old man)
Mt 10:8 is done by Rom 8, and Duet 30:14-16
Fruit isn't works – It's a relationship with Jesus

TWENTY FOUR

Bob's heart and word for the last days.....
So the fifties revealed my power And it came in a mighty way And the sixties revealed my Holy Spirit and the baptism that then began to fall And produce the mighty songs that were lifted up to me. And the seventies began to reveal the great teachers And this is where many of you I began to bring forth to me In the seventies my teachers began to bring my word For my kingdom is based upon my word and my Spirit These are the two pillars that I started back in the seventies. The eighties revealed the Spirit of God and my prophets .The nineties revealed my government.
And now my government is in place And in a time of great stress I shall bring forth my next step for Toronto was a step Brownsville was another step My next step will be my glory And signs like you have never seen before. And ever since you have You'll see become golden among thee You'll smell the fragrance of heaven You'll taste the goodness of God You'll feel the presence of God and angels in awesome ways You'll hear the songs of heaven and the praise And you'll see the angels and his working mightily Bringing your five senses, sanctifying them So that he can show you himself And all of your soul your way For what I have just described you see is your soul. So yes, he's been dealing in your spirit and he has for a while But now he is after the rest of you, the soul That he might use it to bring a new day So yes, get ready for God's glory.
And the 2010's will bring you see, the faith of God To speak cre-

ative miracles, To change the storms To shut up the heavens or loose up the heavens. And the 2020's you see, that worketh by faith Shall bring a new day And it shall be an army of love And a maturity and a brand new way For it shall be called the family of God Joined together in a unity The most powerful force that the world has ever seen and shall ever see in all her days. And still time will go on For you have time for your children and your grandchildren So don't get in any hurry, for I'm not So I'm calling thee to begin to represent me Be my ambassadors, be my goodwill ambassadors To all the nations upon the earth you see.

For a couple of years ago I began to plow you As an ox does and I began to test you And I began to give you the dullest prayer meetings you have ever seen. And boy you just felt blah I was plowing you, you see For the ox does plow and he knows not why And he grips a little, and that's what you did, you see. But he keeps saying, "I'm plowing all day but there's not a green thing to eat! And I see the old harvest back in the fifties and the other times, yes I see that But there's nothing there to eat! Why is he having me to plow? And every once and awhile I run into this old hard ground. What's that? I think they called it fallow ground. Yes, I've seen what it produced years ago. And yet you just keep saying, 'plow, plow, plow.'"

And for the last few years you see, have been plowing for the ox is my beatitudes. And any movement that I will do will go through my beatitudes Let my beatitudes be your attitudes. You want me to move then let my attitudes dwell in thee For you see I gave you a hunger and a thirst for me And I kept guiding you by my Holy Spirit even both night and day in your barrenness.

So you'll keep plowing and keep getting the demonic roots out of your soul. Doubt, unbelief, not in me so much but in me able to use you For you say, 'You know you'. But I'm going to tell you, you are wrong You don't even know yourself. You have no idea how much I love you And what I paid for you is what you are worth Its the enemy that you agree with when you degrade yourself And so I've been plowing you to plow your thinking up And to plow those things that does so easily entangle thee To get them out of the way that I might have my way with thee And so yes, I've been plowing you to bring you to a place called meekness. For the meek, they shall inherit. For you see, meekness is teachable and those who are teachable my Holy Spirit makes disciples out of them And begins to bring my divine nature into them And so you are my disciple you see, so long as you are teachable And allow me to show you my way.

In my beatitudes in you, I called you to be peacemakers in these last days. For they shall be called my sons and daughters. They shall be close to me But I'm going to tell you what a peacemaker is Its one that can confront the issues and can bring a righteous judgment you see, And the first one that I wanted you to confront is the enemy between your eyes That you would confront those things that does keep you from embracing me Only when you are peaceful within your soul can you rest So that my rest might come into thee and bring you my way so if you are not able to rest And are continually striving, then turn around and sit down and begin to love me And I'll bring you into that place of peace within that you might make peace with yourself For that is what my peacemakers first do you see, Is get rid of all that garbage that the fallen nature has put on thee So that you can come forth and be that son and daughter for me So yes, let my beatitudes be your attitude in me but I do say that now the plowing is coming to an end In Isaiah 28:24 it says that I don't plow all the time you see For I plowed thee for 9 years I broke up your hard hearted nature, the clods And I have smoothed my fields.

And now I am going to cast my seeds into them My sperm seed words will now come to my body And it will begin to grow harvest in different ways Even as there are different things that I sow to bring forth into harvest Will I sow these things in you Different in each one of you for I'm bringing forth the harvest of grain in people That my body might consume This grain that I'm bringing forth Is so that the body can eat your lives up And become a healthy body of Christ.

And in my word, it says that I will show you the wisdom you need for this So yes, I'm sowing you back the remnant seed The drought is over now in the church and it will rain And my God sperm seed I placed in your heart will begin to grow. But the falls of the season you will begin to come forth in an awesome harvest. And you'll begin to see that the grain is out there And it will be where my body can eat your life up And be healthy enough to go into the world and take the lands for me And so the next move of the Spirit you'll see will be the eagle. And my rhema words falling in thee Get ready for vision like you have never seen before. Get ready for my picture For I'm getting ready to give my vision to my body. So that they no longer perish but each and every one of you have a picture, a vision for your life and a purpose in Christ All of you join neatly together for when I crush my grain to feed my body You can't tell one from another I'm going to mix you that well so that you'll just have to say, 'we're just a part of the body of Christ' And we are literally ministry without a face And the face you'll see, is the face of Christ.

Yes, now is my seasons And my eagle you see, is in Mark 16. For I've been going throughout all the earth, Preparing my people to go and obey my commandment. For as I have been bringing you into that meekness So that I could show you then so will I send you as I did my son. So send I you into the world That you will begin to fulfill my great commission And go into all the nations, into all the ethnic groups Of which are right here in this city, Start there. And that you might begin to make disciples of all of the ethnic groups For I will tell you this, my son didn't die on the cross needlessly for the whole world to glorify death and sin in the last days I am going to have the mightiest church you have ever seen and over a billion souls will come in one great wave And all who will can come and find both bread and wine So I am going to begin to give the revelation Especially the revelation of my true common union communion for my body had been fragmented, broken apart And now I will begin to bring it back together For I will begin to pour my wine upon my broken fragmented body And begin to bring it again into one body, one lump. And I say this to you, it won't be grape juice I pour upon it. Because grape juice has no spirit in it It will be the best of my wine with real spirit in it, a wedding wine, a unity wine. And I shall join my body together by my spirit And my blood shall flow through their veins.

For this is the inheritance of the saints you see To not be defeated in the last day I'm not coming for a bride that has been pinched by the devil on the backside, and bruised and defeated and crying out to me. I won't come until that bride does say, "The Holy Spirit and I are ready." And then it will be no surprise for my body for they will be the ones who will send for me and it will be because they are victorious in every way And put on all of my nature And so it will only be a surprise to the world you see, but it won't be a surprise to my body.

I'm not going to cut anything off in the last days. For it grows darker and so shall it grow lighter in thee. And my light shall shine greater and farther in thee. For I am calling forth my body of Christ To walk upon the earth where the very earth itself does tremble at their footsteps. And to where the heathen does tremble at their words Because they will have power over life and death, over storm and fire and all the things of nature, And by their word, by their word, that they speak as they mature in me will there be life or death as they do say, 'rain or drought' That's what will happen as they learn to literally loose my prayers in a brand new way.

But now after you I say, 'a new anointing of my rhema, and binding and losing shall shortly be on thee and you shall begin to loose the yoke of bondage of religion that has held you back in these last days. For a religious spirit is legalism, opinion, debate, judgment and criticism. And none of that is of me for I am of love and they are of works. So these things I do say. You don't have any right to any of these, you have only a right to love and to dwell in my presence both night and day. So yes, a door I open to thee, so walk in it and live your life for me and possess everything that your foot does walk on in these last days.

TWENTY FIVE

Always be aware of attack of a control spirit

Ps 73:15-17 If I had said, "I will speak thus,"

I would have betrayed your children. When I tried to understand all this,

it was oppressive to me till I entered the sanctuary of God;

then I understood their final destiny.

What do we have to be bothered about

7 things

We are: spirit, mental, physical,

We do: Financial, Social, Sexual, And Emotional

Ps 73:28

8 But as for me, it is good to be near God.

I have made the Sovereign LORD my refuge;

I will tell of all your deeds.

The "Religious Spirit"..Many of the prophetic experiences given to Bob involve symbols and imagery of this nature. Whenever spirits of this nature are identified, it is always beneficial to remind ourselves that we contend not against flesh and blood, only against principalities, powers and spiritual wickedness in heavenly places. (Ephesians 6:12)

In a prophetic experience the "religious spirit" was illustrated to Bob with the appearance of the "abominable snowman" yet with the title of "Abominable Snow-job Man". Each word in this description designates attributes of this spirit.

The vision Bob had was to give understanding this spirit is designed to illustrate its abominable quality from the Lord's perspective. To the natural eye the religious spirit attempts to operate so close to the manner of the Holy Spirit that it would be unrecognizable unless spiritually discerned. Thankfully, the Lord is communicating to us distinguishable attributes of this destructive enemy of our souls and the fruit that it bears.

In the vision, Bob was told that this spirit can be found in Isaiah

66:15-18 attempting to lead the people into the Divine Presence by an unlawful means resulting in the Judgement of God. For with fire and with his sword the LORD will execute judgment upon all men, and many will be those slain by the LORD." Those who consecrate and purify themselves to go into the gardens, following the one in the midst of those who eat the flesh of pigs and rats and other abominable things, they will meet their end together," declares the LORD." And I, because of their actions and their imaginations, am about to come and gather all nations and tongues, and they will come and see my glory.

The religious spirit directs the people to sanctify themselves but only in their minds ministering to them the "flesh of swine" and "mice". These two Biblically unclean animals represent unsanctified nourishment presented to the people through the soul of man rather than the Holy Spirit. These could depict intellectual comprehension and opinions of the Scriptures apart from the divine revelation released through the Spirit of Truth. This is abominable in the sight of the Lord.

Unsanctified thoughts and vain imaginations surrender opportunity to the enemy to loose anointed curses through this type administration resulting in persecution and intimidation. The church becomes desolate when this spirit controls and feeds the temple of man.

The religious spirit introduces into the Church the spirit of the world nullifying the Grace of God. The views of Truth necessary to purify the church are not such as the world gives, but are such as are communicated by the Spirit of God. This spirit will attempt to lead the Church away from the reality of God expressed in the Book of Acts.

In the vision Bob saw what initially appeared to be an angel with female appearances descending from heaven. As the image advanced closer he saw a name written upon her—EKKLESIA–"Called Out Ones". Close observation revealed that she had neither hands nor feet. This expressed that the proper biblical priesthood had not yet been released to the body to prepare her for unimpaired bridal duties. The Lord indicated that He was going to release the "Zadok" priesthood to teach the distinction between the clean and the profane. (Ezekiel 44:15-16) This ministry will be the government of God providing a cleansing light purifying her to emerge as the glorious bride of Christ.

The Spirit then declared that He is calling forth His "reserves" to active duty. These reserves can be found in (Jeremiah 50:20). In those days, and in that time, saith the LORD, the iniquity of Israel shall be sought for, and there shall be none; and the sins of Judah, and they shall not be found: for I will pardon them whom I reserve.

To these "Pardoned Ones" the Lord is going to equip with the authority of the "Rod of Iron" to serve as a bridge over troubled waters. The Holy Spirit will function as a bridge of deliverance leading to Calvary's Cross. Reserves are defined as a military force withheld for the use by a commander when he desires to commit those troops decisively to battle and enemy engagement. These will also be anointed with the Lord's "battle axe" for the purpose of laying the axe to the root of the religious tree.

The apostle Paul identified the religious spirit in (2 Corinthians 11:12-15). But what I am doing, I will continue to do, that I may cut off opportunity from those who desire an opportunity to be regarded just as we are in the matter about which they are boasting. For such men are false apostles, deceitful workers, disguising themselves as apostles of Christ. And no wonder, for even Satan disguises himself as an angel of light. Therefore it is not surprising if his servants also disguise themselves as servants of righteousness; whose end shall be according to their deeds.

It is the gospel of the glory of Christ that is the greatest threat to the kingdom of darkness and it is this very gospel that must be demonstrated during this generation to bring the bride to the point of perfection. For God who said "light shall shine out of darkness, is the One who has shone in our hearts to give the light of the KNOWLEDGE OF THE GLORY OF GOD IN THE FACE OF CHRIST. (2 Corinthians 4:6)

TWENTY SIX

Self-pity strongest negative spirit in the Body of Christ – it opens door to demonic activity – it focuses on past – blame shifting (not taking responsibility for your own sin).

focus on self nullifies the cross

Selfishness separates you from God

He cannot move in your life

When the enemy reminds you of your past, REMIND HIM OF HIS FUTURE

You can curse yourself with your eyes when you look in the mirror

bless yourself daily

Reject timidity and fear

Don't panic – laugh at panic

Children of Israel shoes didn't ware out and didn't get sick. They were disobedient, no faith, complained – How much more will the Lord give us.

Purpose of wilderness – hear His voice

Learn how to respond to His voice

Cancer - curse rebellious cells..Will blow up first when dying – then collapses(after few days)

Paradise is for the nominal

Christian – the throne room is for the overcomer

Command the blessings to come in

The church is being challenged by the Holy Spirit in this hour to take our position of authority to rebuke influenza and the spread of various other diseases in our nation. In a vision, Bob saw the enemy's plan to spread fever and other illnesses through mosquitoes. The day has now arrived when we must openly, on a regular basis release the authority of the Lord's blood as a shield against these onslaughts.

Zechariah 9 depicts a battle between the sons of Zion and the sons of Greece. This prophetic portrayal is a clear representation of this next season of the spirit. The storm winds of the South over the past year highlight the inauguration of this spiritual conflict.

The sons of Zion are called to a place of intimate fellowship with the Lord. They will possess an anointing like the one that rested upon the sons of Zadok. Their call will be first to minister unto the Lord and His affection. From that place of fellowship, this company will begin to sift the clean from the unclean and separate the precious from the profane.

Ezekiel 44:16 & 23

They shall enter My sanctuary; they shall come near to My table to minister to Me and keep My charge...Moreover, they shall teach My people the difference between the holy and the profane, and cause them to discern between the unclean and the clean.

"Lord, don't let me have my own way"

Uzzah – arm of the flesh – breech – he touched the Ark of the Covenant

Walking in the prophetic – be teachable, meek – ask God for understanding

See it and obey

Mercy – not getting what I deserve

Grace – getting what I don't deserve

Independence – Lawlessness

Bubbles and white circles in photos are angels

Speaking and singing in tongues – El Shaddai (the many breasted one)

Dedicated line to God – nursing(living tissue) on the Fathers breast – His heart

THE REMNANT SEED COMING FORTH

TWENTY-SEVEN

BOB SPOKE THIS AROUND 2005

God's people are the remnant seed. The Lord is getting ready to sow again the remnant of His people. Many Christians are literally in a time of death to self; the seed of God is sown with travail and weeping. One of the main delays has simply been waiting on the Lord's timing. God has timing for His plans. He has been working on and empowering many people for years in preparation for this hour.

It has been long and difficult but God has given us new life at different times to encourage us to continue to press into Him. He gave us Toronto bringing back the joy. He gave us Brownsville bringing with an emphasis on repentance. The Lord has allowed the Church other expressions of His grace to bring us to this point. Now the Lord of the Harvest has arisen. Everyone is called to have a role in the harvest; harvest begins with prayer. According to Job 22:30, the Lord will even deliver the one for whom you intercede who is not innocent. He will be delivered through the cleanness of your hands.

When you pray, begin first in your own family; pray for those who are not innocent and who do not have clean hands and have not yet embraced the Lord's salvation and perhaps given you the worst counsel. That is what Job did.

It came about after the LORD had spoken these words to Job, that the LORD said to Eliphaz the Temanite, "My wrath is kindled against you and against your two friends because you have not spoken of Me what is right as My servant Job has. Now, therefore, take for yourselves seven bulls and seven rams, and go to My servant Job, and offer up a burnt offering for yourselves, and My servant Job will pray for you. For I will accept him so that I may not do with you according to your folly, because you have not spoken of Me what is right, as My servant Job has...The LORD restored the fortunes of Job when he prayed for his friends, and the LORD increased all that Job had twofold. (Job 42:7-8 & 10)

The righteous prayer of Job intervened for those around him despite their folly. It is time the fortune of God's people be restored as well. The Lord turned the captivity of Job and restored double his fortune when he prayed for his friends. We are entering the season of the double-portion.

The eyes of the Lord are roving to and fro looking for a righteous agency on the earth to stand in the gap. The Lord is asking, "is there no man when I call? Is there anyone to answer? I am speaking is there anyone listening? Is my hand shortened at all that it cannot redeem? Or have I no power to deliver? Don't you know who I am?"

There will be a remnant of people on the earth who hear and respond to this call. According to Isaiah 50:2 the Lord asked,

Why was there no man when I came? When I called, why was there none to answer? Is My hand so short that it cannot ransom? Or have I no power to deliver? Behold, I dry up the sea with My rebuke, I make the rivers a wilderness; their fish stink for lack of water and die of thirst.

Command the blessings to come!! Don't let the enemy destroy you. Embrace Joy, it's your lifeline

Anxiety destroys your immune system.

I saw a skirt covered with pillbugs – distractions, busyness, and survival – thoughts not Christ-centered SHAKE THEM OFF. Ask God what to pray and pray it. Don't plan apart from the Holy Spirit. Resist doubt and unbelief

The Lord can change things quickly. He is giving His people an instructed tongue that we may sustain the weary with a word from Him. He is presently awakening many saints morning by morning that He may give to them eyes to see and ears to hear as His disciples.

Isa 52:2

2 Shake off your dust;
rise up, sit enthroned, O Jerusalem.
Free yourself from the chains on your neck,
O captive Daughter of Zion.

Many in the Church are coming to the end of a season of pruning and judgment as it is beginning in the world. His desire is for our light to shine brightly for many people will be heading our way in the great night. It is time for those who overcome to arise with a measure of His glory resting on them. This will literally be the season for the fulfillment of Daniel's prophecy when he wrote,

Those who have insight will shine brightly like the brightness of the expanse of heaven, and those who lead the many to righteousness, like the stars forever and ever (Daniel 12:3)

This is the time for the accomplishment of divine purposes and a wave of harvest. The Lord is laying claim to this generation of young people as well as the seasoned and mature. It will be both the Joshua's and the Caleb's. The Lord is healing the fracture He has created in a third-day harvest of the wounded and persecuted. His will is being accomplished in a mighty way so that a harvest can be achieved.

The trials in the earth will increase in an awesome way while at the same time the end-time truths from the book of Revelations shall become increasingly clear. Great understanding will be delegated to the Church concerning these mysteries.

The book of Revelations is a love letter to the Lord's bride and prepares her to be joined to Him. He is calling to those with ears to hear what He is saying concerning these times and seasons. This will not be a time to do anything presumptuously, but those who are led by the Spirit can rest in His protection and grace.

The Lord has already triumphed over the adversary and made a public spectacle of him. Now is the time for us to comprehend more fully that reality and appropriate it. The Lord is delegating His victory to us when we are joined to Him.

One of our greatest callings in this hour is to no longer be considered the Lord's servants, but His friends. We have a Friend who is eternally positioned on His throne of victory and authority and we need a more complete vision of this to fully activate our faith. Commissioning from the throne room can be a living reality as promised through God's word. He is saying "come up here!"

He is calling His Church to discern the times and know the seasons and to know the mind of Christ for this day. It isn't His desire to hide it from us but reveal great understanding so that the heathen may see God's blessing and wisdom upon His people. That is what the grooming of the last decade has been intended to accomplish. The pain of our past is the preparation for our future.

TWENTY EIGHT

Sometimes sitting listening to Bob he would begin to prophecy.
THIS WAS RECORDED

"The '80's revealed my prophets you see And the '90's revealed my government and my justice Even improving upon this day. But now my heart cries in another way. For I will now raise up my shepherds And my shepherds will love the sheep My shepherds you see will die for the sheep they will stand between the enemy and my body. For now, I work on bringing forth my body. I have brought forth my head. My leadership I have already got upon the earth and my purpose now you see is for my leadership to feed my body. For my body is like a baby and my leadership is like a grown head upon a baby's body.

So everything I do now in my leadership will be to feed my body of Christ So that they may grow up and possess the gates of the enemy for have I not said continually in my word That their children would inherit the earth And the earth in that day, When my justice comes in a mighty way will bless them For I will only destroy the world you see and its corruption but the earth will remain and I will bless it. And your children will inherit it. So you must learn my word and believe it you see. For have I not said, 'that once I was young but now I am old' but I have never seen the righteous forsaken or his seed begging for bread.

So I call you to a new intimacy with me a new covenant with me that you quit doing all those things that you are doing and do only that which you see with me. So I've called you to open the eyes of your heart, and the ears of your understanding and your discernment and your love for me. So that our love can be upon the earth again in these last days.

For you see my shepherds will be shepherds of love. They will not harm the sheep. For they have failed so much they have learned to love. They have been broken so they know what brokenness is. And my sheep will know me. Each one will know me and my voice in this last day. So the good shepherd is coming into your life you see. To make you lay down and be still in green pastures. And make your soul be still and know that he is God And yes, my good shepherds that are coming out of the backwoods, out of the slums, out of many places, They will put to rest the troubled waters in the church They will still the waters in the church They will have the authority to speak against those that lie The gossips the slanderers, Those that trouble the waters of the church They will put them silent and they will bring the still waters. So that my sheep, my body may drink deep of me.

For I say this day, that I call forth deep unto deep. And I shall bring thee by the new way that you know not. So get ready for my power to see In an awesome new way, And it will be called forth by prophecy Get ready for the creative word of God to come forth through my prophets. This is according to scripture you see Isaiah 48:6-7 is what it says, For I am still a creative God And when I give my word to my children, and to my prophets and they proclaim it upon the earth It comes to pass you see.

For three years ago a great famine in the south west of the United States did reign over all the land. And I spoke to a prophet and I told him to command, proclaim rain. To not pray for it you see but to proclaim it and to command the angels to bring rain. And three times on a Sunday this was done you see. I doubt that many understood in any way but they know this that within three days, it rained 7 inches in places that hadn't seen rain for 3 years. That's proclaiming you see, That's agreeing with God And speaking his words that he wants proclaimed So yes intercede, seek God but once you hear Proclaim, command So when you drive your streets in your cities Pray over them And wait for my word to come to thee So that you might speak into the heart of that city and bring forth life. And so this has happened often lately But is shall happen even more now that the times have become even more severe you see. So if you don't like the tornado coming your way lose the angels and command it to split And this has happened before you see. So it's time that my church rises up and become my body My body of Christ. That takes the authority that I've given you see.

For I didn't make you pussycats, I made you lions. I made you to take the prey in these last days I made you to take those who are your enemies to fall away to thee when I give you the words. I'm getting you ready for my fire and the baptism of fire, which is a spirit of holiness, which is the fruit of the spirit maturing you up. For you do not cry out for revival but you cry for more and more every day for my mercy and my grace and my light. For I have come to this area to stay. I didn't come for my glory to pass away and fade as it has in past days. I've come for my glory to abide upon thee continually and to rest upon your children in eternity for it is the last days but it is not immediately. You'll see the 2000's, the 2010's, 2020's, and 2030's. So make long-range plans. Yep.

For I tell you, you're not going to fly away right away. But your coming and going to raise up the body of Christ that will inherit, And that my glory will abide upon thee And sickness, sin and poverty will not be able to stand in your presence you see. And the gods that men have worshiped will fall down and bow down to thee Including doctors and lawyers and psychologists and philosophers. They shall come to acknowledge me in thee.

For these 9 years, I worked in thee was to root out the things that displeased me. So I sent you into the desert after awaking thee and you carried all of your baggage with you. So the first couple of years you began to throw some of it away. The next couple of years you threw a little more away. You kept on going until all you had left you see Was a couple of water jugs and your idols of gold; your ideas of what you wanted done in me. The last couple of years I have just been working beautifully in thee. Your golden ideas and idols lay out there in the desert you see. All you've got left is a water bottle and it's less than a third full; so I had you shedding. When you thought you were going to die out there you decided to pray and try it my way and that's where your prayer is at today. In your desperation, you began to pray. Not until you had to, that is, not until you couldn't figure it out.

So now I've called you to think it out in these last days and now I will give you my mind and show you my way and you'll not fail anymore. I'm not in my church failures in any way. I'm in my son's growth in bringing him forth to inherit you see. Even now men and women in this body, in the time of exchange of great finances, I'm raising him up to possess and give millions into my evangelism and into my church. I'm going to let them spoil Egypt again. Not only Egypt but the world system of marketing. Even now, I'm moving upon the minds of men and women and giving them this knowledge. In their heart for me will be to see my word exported over all the earth in these last days. And so the fifties, the 19 and 50's What goes around comes back around you see So the anointing of the 50's is coming back your way. So the 50's reveal my power That's coming back your way but I'll not give my power to any that have not shed the things that displease me And unresolved anger is one of the things that greatly displeases me And that's what I've been doing in thee this day To get the unresolved anger out of you that my glory might rest upon you So that no root of bitterness or anything might defile many if I anointed thee with my glory.

So the fifties revealed my power And it came in a mighty way And the sixties revealed my Holy Spirit and the baptism that then began to fall And produce the mighty songs that were lifted up to me. And the seventies began to reveal the great teachers And this is where many of you I began to bring forth to me In the seventies my teachers began to bring my word For my kingdom is based upon my word and my Spirit These are the two pillars that I started back in the seventies. The eighties revealed the Spirit of God and my prophets. The nineties revealed my government.

And now my government is in place And in a time of great stress I shall bring forth my next step for Toronto was a step Brownsville was another step My next step will be my glory And signs like you have never seen before. And ever since you have You'll see become golden among thee You'll smell the fragrance of heaven

You'll taste the goodness of God You'll feel the presence of God and angels in awesome ways You'll hear the songs of heaven and the praise And you'll see the angels and his working mightily Bringing your five senses, sanctifying them So that he can show you himself And all of your soul your way For what I have just described you see is your soul. So yes, he's been dealing in your spirit and he has for a while But now he is after the rest of you, the soul That he might use it to bring a new day So yes, get ready for God's glory.

And the 2010's will bring you see, the faith of God To speak creative miracles, To change the storms To shut up the heavens or loose up the heavens. And the 2020's you see, that worketh by faith Shall bring a new day And it shall be an army of love And a maturity and a brand new way For it shall be called the family of God Joined together in a unity The most powerful force that the world has ever seen and shall ever see in all her days. And still, time will go on For you have time for your children and your grandchildren So don't get in any hurry, for I'm not So I'm calling thee to begin to represent me Be my ambassadors, be my goodwill ambassadors To all the nations upon the earth you see.

For a couple of years ago, I began to plow you As an ox does and I began to test you And I began to give you the dullest prayer meetings you have ever seen. And boy you just felt blah I was plowing you, you see For the ox does plow and he knows not why And he grips a little, and that's what you did, you see. But he keeps saying, "I'm plowing all day but there's not a green thing to eat! And I see the old harvest back in the fifties and the other times, yes I see that But there's nothing there to eat! Why is he having me to plow? And every once and awhile I run into this old hard ground. What's that? I think they called it fallow ground. Yes, I've seen what it produced years ago. And yet you just keep saying, 'plow, plow, plow.'"

And for the last few years you see, have been plowing for the ox is my beatitudes. And any movement that I will do will go through my beatitudes Let my beatitudes be your attitudes. You want me to move then let my attitudes dwell in thee For you see I gave you a hunger and a thirst for me And I kept guiding you by my Holy Spirit even both night and day in your barrenness.

So you'll keep plowing and keep getting the demonic roots out of your soul. Doubt, unbelief, not in me so much but in me able to use you For you say, 'You know you'. But I'm going to tell you, you are wrong You don't even know yourself. You have no idea how much I love thee And what I paid for you is what you are worth Its the enemy that you agree with when you degrade yourself And so I've been plowing you to plow your thinking up And to plow those things that does so easily entangle thee To get them out of the way that I might have my way with thee And so yes, I've been plowing you to bring you to a place called meekness. For the meek, they shall inherit. For you see, meekness is teachable and those who are teachable my Holy Spirit makes disciples out of them And begins to bring my divine nature into them And so you are my disciple you see, so long as you are teachable And allow me to show you my way.

In my beatitudes in thee, I called you to be peacemakers in these last days. For they shall be called my sons and daughters. They shall be close to me But I'm going to tell you what a peacemaker is Its one that can confront the issues and can bring a righteous judgment you see, And the first one that I wanted you to confront is the enemy between your eyes That you would confront those things that does keep you from embracing me Only when you are peaceful within your soul can you rest So that my rest might come into thee and bring you my way so if you are not able to rest And are continually striving, then turn around and sit down and begin to love me And I'll bring you into that place of peace within that you might make peace with yourself For that is what my peacemakers first do you see, Is get rid of all that garbage that the fallen nature has put on thee So that you can come forth and be that son and daughter for me So yes, let my beatitudes be your attitude in me but I do say that now the plowing is coming to an end In Isaiah 28:24 it says that I don't plow all the time you see For I plowed thee for 9 years I broke up your hard hearted nature, the clods And I have smoothed my fields.

And now I am going to cast my seeds into them My sperm seed words will now come to my body And it will begin to grow harvest in different ways Even as there are different things that I sow to bring forth into harvest Will I sow these things in thee Different in each one of thee for I'm bringing forth the harvest of grain in people That my body might consume This grain that I'm bringing forth Is so that the body can eat your lives up And become a healthy body of Christ.

And in my word, it says that I will show you the wisdom you need for this So yes, I'm sowing you back the remnant seed The drought is over now in the church and it will rain And my God sperm seed I placed in your heart will begin to grow. But the falls of the season you will begin to come forth in an awesome harvest. And you'll begin to see that the grain is out there And it will be where my body can eat your life up And be healthy enough to go into the world and take the lands for me And so the next move of the Spirit you'll see will be the eagle. And my rhema words falling in thee Get ready for vision like you have never seen before. Get ready for my picture For I'm getting ready to give my vision to my body. So that they no longer perish but each and every one of you have a picture, a vision for your life and a purpose in Christ All of you join neatly together for when I crush my grain to feed my body You can't tell one from another I'm going to mix you that well so that you'll just have to say, 'we're just a part of the body of Christ' And we are literally ministry without a face And the face you'll see, is the face of Christ.

But now after you, I say, 'a new anointing of my rhema, and binding and losing shall shortly be on thee and you shall begin to lose the yoke of bondage of religion that has held you back in these last days. For a religious spirit is legalism, opinion, debate, judgment, and criticism. And none of that is of me for I am of love and they are of works. So these things I do say. You don't have any right to any of these, you have only a right to love and to dwell in my presence both night and day. So yes, a door I open to thee, so walk in it and live your life for me and possess everything that your foot does walk on in these last days."

TWENTY NINE

Bob loved to talk about angel incounters.

He would say that angels were assigned to us at birth and are with us throughout our life yet often times we don't see them. Angels escort us home to the Lord at the end of life's journey.

Psalms 91:11 says that God commands His angels to protect, defend and guard us in all our ways. I believe these are "watcher angels" that simply watch over us all of our life. And when we're about to encounter something dangerous this angel instructs other ones to prevent its occurrence. Can you remember a time when you just missed being struck by another vehicle or perhaps dodged a falling object? Do you remember how many people were detained for one reason or another on 9/11 that prevented their arrival at the twin towers? Angels on assignment will cause you to stay out of harm's way.

Bob depended on angels to assist him in ministry. Often times you would hear him say, "Feel the wind"? He was talking about angels. Hebrews 1:7 says, And concerning the angels He says, "Who makes His angels winds, and His ministering servants flames of fire (to do His bidding)." They are the wind and we are the fire and together we get the job done through obedience to the Father. Because Psalms 103:20 says, Bless the Lord, you His angels, you mighty ones who do His commandments, obeying the voice of His word! I always admired how Bob would wait to hear from the Holy Spirit what needed to be done in ministry. He didn't just jump the gun or shoot from the hip so to speak. He waited till he heard what was necessary for healing, a miracle or deliverance then he spoke. And the angels ministered with him.

He had two mighty angels named Emma and Grace that often traveled with him. He said their name is their job description; Emma means healing while Grace worked miracles. They made a mighty team. Yet many he called "Tinkerbells" because they are like small twinkling lights or fireflies. Often they show up as a confirmation to the truth of a prophetic word or that an assignment has been completed. Many times people have thought they "never" see angels but they see little twinkling lights. These are angels too but they have lesser assignments.

Bob described many experiences with angels, but this one about Emma was over the top.

He told me that Emma was the angel that helped birth and start the whole prophetic movement in Kansas City in the 1980s. She was a mothering-type angel that helped nurture the prophetic as it broke out.

She floated a couple of inches off the floor. It was almost like Kathryn Khulman in those old videos when she wore a white dress and looked like she was gliding across the platform. Emma appeared beautiful and young-about 22 years old-but she was old at the same time. She seemed to carry the wisdom, virtue and grace of Proverbs 31 on her life.

She glided into the room, emitting brilliant light and colors. Emma carried these bags and began pulling gold out of them. Then, as she walked up and down the aisles of the church, she began putting gold dust on people. "God, what is happening?" I asked. The Lord answered: "She is releasing the gold, which is both the revelation and the financial breakthrough that I am bringing into this church. I want you to prophecy that Emma showed up in this service-the same angel that appeared in Kansas city-as a sign that I am endorsing and releasing a prophetic spirit in the church." See, when angels come, they always come for a reason; we need to actually ask God what the purpose is.

THIRTY

You are Sons and Daughters

You are children of your Father

Judgment is all around us... Anxiety, Fear, and Panic

In this time of great pressure, we're all seeking a secret hiding place where we can be safe. Bob had a vision that Shangri-La was real and is on the earth today. A city not made by hands but by God. Seek to enter into His REST. There is a way or a path that leads up the mountains to the valley of Shangri-La. The way, of course, is Christ Jesus and the mountain we climb is Psalm 24:3&4.

Who may ascend into the hill of the LORD? Or who may stand in His holy place? He who has clean hands and a pure heart, Who has not lifted up his soul to an idol, Nor sworn deceitfully. (Psalm 24:3-4)

As we climb into that mountain we come to a door or pass and Christ is that door. In that city is a place of peace and rest where there is no sickness but the blessings of God are over that city. He's given us the direction on how to climb the mountain of God so we can find that place of peace and rest within our soul.

For truly our soul never dies and there's eternal life forever. There's a place on the earth now that we can flee from the judgments that have started and have peace and rest in our soul. Jesus Christ is the Way and the Door and those who find Him will find peace beyond all understanding. They will be hidden from the judgments in Jesus Christ.

(Isaiah 26:20) says Come, my people, enter your chambers, and shut your doors behind you; Hide yourself, as it were, for a little moment, Until the indignation is past.

Jesus Christ is the only absolute down here and He is the Shangri-La that we must flee to; that city made by God.

If you are going to be self-centered, then you make room for some of this stuff to come into you.

But if you get Christ-centered it isn't there..

It is illegal to have this stuff. You're not entitled to them. It is sin.

Fear is having a big devil and a little bitty God. You are not entitled to fear.

When these things come against us we need to tell them to shut up...take action against these things.

We need to learn the spiritual language of the Holy Spirit and talk to God all the time.

Recently the Lord said, "We must take an aggressive stand against spoken words." It gives the enemy permission to act on their behalf. We must cancel the power and authority of the spoken word! Any place that we leave an opening the enemy will use it to his advantage. Words have the power to bless or curse.

We must cancel the power and authority of any spoken word that is not lined up with God's divine will and purpose for our destiny in the kingdom of God. I pray daily for our families; canceling the power and authority of spoken words that are contrary to God's divine will and purpose for our destiny in Him. Then I release blessings and favor for it is God's will for us to prosper in all things both spiritual and natural.

The enemy does not know our thoughts; only God does. However, the enemy provokes our thoughts to get us off track and agree with him or simply "buy the lie." He'll provoke us to remember things that we've already repented of and bring condemnation. He will play with our thoughts and get us to question "truth" and operate in doubt and unbelief instead of faith. And he'll twist words so that we hear the opposite of what is spoken and become prey to the accuser. Once we fall prey to the enemy's tactics and allow our thoughts to form spoken words, we become the devil's advocate. Our words begin swirling looking for a place to land. (Psalm 34:13) Keep your tongue from evil, and your lips from speaking deceit.

The key words in this are AGGRESSIVE STAND and PERMISSION. We must take our every thought captive and bring it into the obedience of Jesus Christ by standing on the word of God in a place of God like faith. Otherwise, we give the enemy permission to use them against us. We allow him to do his will according to our free will or the choice we make.

Often times we speak words against ourselves. We know our own pitfalls – so does the enemy. When we hear the lie in our conscience we must cast them down immediately and not agree with them by speaking them out. We are the prophet of our own life; speak blessings not curses.

We must bridle our tongues. (James 3:3-4) says a bit is set in the horses' mouths to make them obey; it will turn their whole body. Large ships driven by rough winds are steered by a very small rudder at the impulse of the helmsman's determination.

Every day I begin prayer for the United States by canceling the power and authority of all words spoken by anyone in political power (including news media) that are contrary to the will of God for this Nation. Our nation has a destiny in God. I ask for the Spirit of Truth to be revealed and preside over our Nation.

THIRTY ONE

In a dream Bob saw the Lord releasing a deposit of His glory to the earth. This was a very specific gift of God's goodness for this next season of the Spirit.

In the midst of the glory that was coming he saw a golden eagle descending from heaven with the unfolding of God's favor. Very often prophetic releases of God's purposes are represented by a bald eagle. However, it was very important to recognize that this was emblematic of a golden eagle representing a very unique quality of God's attributes.

The Golden Eagle

In the experience it was clear that the golden eagle was specially equipped to eradicate the spiritual influences represented by a serpent...specifically a king cobra. Much of the Egyptian mysticism centered on this serpent and the unholy strongholds it represented. For us, the king cobra has been a symbol of religious spirits set against the high purposes of Heaven.

The golden eagle has also represented apostolic authority in many of the revelations the Lord has given to us. This next season of the spirit beginning this year will see a substantially increased measure of apostolic authority to deal with and eliminate a false anointing that has hindered our quest for the harvest of the ages.

Jesus himself identified this spirit in Matthew 24 as one so close to the real that it would deceive the very elect if it were possible. This is a form of religious spirit that masquerade's as the Holy Spirit but denies the power of God and focuses on works rather than grace. God is much more concerned about what we are becoming than what we are doing. Both are important, however, but our emphasis is first and foremost placed upon becoming more like Him and a reflection of His nature and character.

Removing the Curses

This grace and glory that is being released will provide an authority to remove anointed curses that have been released against churches and fellowships. Very often these curses are imposed from the pulpit by speakers who unknowingly speak from a wounded soul. This can give access to a religious spirit whose ultimate purpose is to frustrate God's plan for the fellowship. Naturally, no one would knowingly do such a thing. However, this form of deception is so subtle that well developed discernment is essential to identify it.

When a curse of this nature is released it opens the door for demonic influences to keep things stirred up in a church or fellowship. Very often divisions, jealousies, strife and other such attributes are sown to keep the body from progressing into the high calling of God.

The religious spirit also promotes fear in people's hearts in lieu of faith. The book of Jude is a clear portrayal of this nemesis and its identifiable fruit. It will emphasize the enemy's ability to deceive us more so than God's great ability to empower us. That is not to imply that we are to be ignorant involving our adversary's plans. We are to be as wise as serpents but as harmless as doves in this regard.

The Lord is determining to lift these demonic assignments that have provided a ceiling on churches and fellowships in their quest for God.

Seven— The Number of Completion

The revelations also drew our attention to something that we initially outlined in the Shepherd's Rod 2004. We will include a portion of those revelations as a matter of emphasis for the days ahead.

In a visionary experience, Bob saw a map of the United States with the number seven (7) superimposed over the map. This was to spiritually indicate that a work of completion had been accomplished in a number of people prepared for a fresh release from Heaven's throne. The places that the number seven laid across the map indicated a unique release of the Spirit in those areas.

That is not to indicate that it is the exclusive place in which the Lord is releasing a deposit of His Spirit. Rather, it is strictly highlighting this area for an extraordinary expression of God to be demonstrated by those specifically prepared for this purpose.

The emblem of the seven seemed to begin along the Gulf coast and expand at an angle toward the northeast with the region of New Hampshire forming the upper most portion of the numerical symbol. From there it extended across the northern portion of the United States and Canada to the West Coast and made a slight turn down around Oregon and California.

There is a finished work that has been fulfilled in a body of people who will be brought close to the Lord and His throne to hear fresh expressions from His heart. Seven is the number symbolic of completion to indicate the maturing that has transpired in those to be used by the Holy Spirit.

As the vision continued, Bob also saw another numerical seven; however, this one was inverted. This was also to indicate the completed and maturing work that has been accomplished in the realm of darkness through those who oppose the work of the cross and the Church of the Lord Jesus.

Our adversary has been at work in a body of people to equip them in the realms of darkness to oppose the fresh dimension of Heaven being unleashed in this hour. The Lord indicated that His Light will always overcome darkness and we should not be threatened by this increased opposition. When we submit ourselves to Him in complete trust, He will go before us in the battle.

Amplified Lust

Unfortunately, the visions continued to illustrate acceleration in the lust of this world for those who are separated from Christ and the destiny of Heaven. These would include the lust of the flesh, the lust of the eyes and the pride of life. The enemy will fuel the passions of the world for "girls, gold and glory." Naturally these three "g's" are a symbolic representation of the snares of the adversary utilized to entrap man by the spirit of this world.

Wickedness will be elevated to a much higher level than even now present. This is the inverted seven that was seen in the previous vision involving the escalation of darkness. The distribution, availability and communication of corruption will only grow worse, if that is imaginable. Our commission is to bring divine light to help lead the many from this overwhelming darkness. It is our time to begin to shine with the brightness of God in order to respond to the elevation in darkness.

Exercising Our Authority

The church is being challenged by the Holy Spirit in this hour to take our position of authority to rebuke influenza and the spread of various other diseases in our nation. In a vision Bob saw the enemy's plan to spread fever and other illnesses through mosquitoes. The day has now arrived when we must openly, on a regular basis release the authority of the Lord's blood as a shield against these onslaughts.

Zechariah 9 depicts a battle between the sons of Zion and the sons of Greece. This prophetic portrayal is a clear representation of this next season of the spirit. The storm winds of the South over the past year highlight the inauguration of this spiritual conflict.

The sons of Zion are called to a place of intimate fellowship with the Lord. They will possess an anointing like the one that rested upon the sons of Zadok. Their call will be first to minister unto the Lord and His affection. From that place of fellowship, this company will begin to sift the clean from the unclean and separate the precious from the profane.

They shall enter My sanctuary; they shall come near to My table to minister to Me and keep My charge...Moreover, they shall teach My people the difference between the holy and the profane, and cause them to discern between the unclean and the clean. (Ezekiel 44:16 & 23)

THIRTY TWO

Watcher Angels are getting ready to appear. They open portals (doors), they show what will happen and they want to help your destiny

Dan 4:13,17,23 "In the visions I saw while lying in my bed, I looked, and there before me was a messenger, a holy one, coming down from heaven. 17 "'The decision is announced by messengers, the holy ones declare the verdict, so that the living may know that the Most High is sovereign over the kingdoms of men and gives them to anyone he wishes and sets over them the lowliest of men.' 23 "You, O king, saw a messenger, a holy one, coming down from heaven and saying, 'Cut down the tree and destroy it, but leave the stump, bound with iron and bronze, in the grass of the field, while its roots remain in the ground. Let him be drenched with the dew of heaven; let him live like the wild animals, until seven times pass by for him.'

Jer 31:28 Just as I watched over them to uproot and tear down, and to overthrow, destroy and bring disaster, so I will watch over them to build and to plant," declares the LORD. PROCLAIM THE KINGDOM.....SPEAK IT INTO EXISTENCE......SEERVE THE LORD WITH JOY AND GLADNESS..... Or you will serve your enemies and they will consume you ..

Sowing is vital! We must sow! Do not eat your seed...sow it!!!

Giving and sowing is a must in order to build the Kingdom of God! Betrayal is your greatest testing of compassion. The greater the violation...the betrayal...the greater the compassion!

The highest anointing brings the highest danger. Healings are a testimony of the Spirit of Prophecy which is the Spirit of Jesus.

Deuteronomy 12:5

5) But you are to seek the place the LORD your God will choose from among all your tribes to put his name there for His dwelling. To that place you must go. The Lord wants to put His name on cities for refuge. When you dwell in the presence of the Lord you get healthier. Only one healing was initiated by Jesus, all others were asked for. Authority inspired priesthood speaks by revelation.

Overcome betrayal and hurt with words with forgiveness. Let go of resentment.

Use the spiritual authority you are given – you are held accountable.

There are 22 portals in the new testament and 300 in Old testament. Speaking in tongues opens portals

The heart of God is for the destitute, the down and out, the hopeless, the poor

Believe God for creative miracles. Always go to doctor Jesus first

When driving – Always ask for divine protection.... Take up your sword of the spirit – get violent. The violent take the Kingdom by force... The force is with you.... The Holy Spirit.... There are treasures to be found in darkness.

Travail until Christ is formed in you.... Amos 9:11-15 "In that day I will restore David's fallen tent. I will repair its broken places, restore its ruins, and build it as it used to be, 12 so that they may possess the remnant of Edom and all the nations that bear my name," declares the LORD, who will do these things. 13 "The days are coming," declares the LORD, "when the reaper will be overtaken by the plowman and the planter by the one treading grapes. New wine will drip from the mountains and flow from all the hills. 14 I will bring back my exiled people Israel; they will rebuild the ruined cities and live in them. They will plant vineyards and drink their wine; they will make gardens and eat their fruit. 15 I will plant Israel in their own land, never again to be uprooted from the land I have given them," says the LORD your God. Only one healing was initiated by Jesus; all others were asked for Zech 4:7-9 "What are you, O mighty mountain? Before Zerubbabel you will become level ground. Then he will bring out the capstone to shouts of 'God bless it! God bless it!'" 8 Then the word of the LORD came to me: 9 "The hands of Zerubbabel have laid the foundation of this temple; his hands will also complete it. Then you will know that the LORD Almighty has sent me to you.

Authority inspired priesthood speaks by revelation.

Pray with (wait) the Lord, not to Him

Isa 11:5 Righteousness will be his belt and faithfulness the sash around his waist.

Commitment. We get where we are going by commitment. Some religious people will not change and they will not get healed. Isaiah 11:11-The second time around! God holds His hand out for me...for us...for the second time around.

Our ceiling must be the floor for our youth!

The outer court yields divine healing.

The inner court yields divine health.

The Holy of Holies yields Divine life.

If God gives you a vision, don't run with it until you get the provision! Get before the Lord and ask for the provision!

THIRTY-THREE

I remember Bob talking about the dead bones..... in 2008

Bob had a vision of the church in a battle, and warfare. It was thrown into a grave with dead bones. Then he heard the audible voice of God saying SOZO. Means healing, Body, Soul, and Spirit. It is time to touch the dead bones and crawl out of your graves.

Bob also began telling a experience of when he was told to go to Spokane, WA and lay his hands on a pine tree. He was ministering in Seattle and he asked a guy if he knew anything special about a pine tree in Spokane. He said yes. At John G Lakes grave there is a pine tree growing out of it. So Bob went to the grave and laid his hands on the pine tree. He said fire came upon his shoulders and hands. He asked the Lord what does this mean. The Lord said the roots go down to the bones. We are to touch those anointed bones of the past. Bob wanted to help us understand his take on our time here on earth... He began telling us about a prophecy he gave.

The 1950's reveal the power of God....Oral Roberts, William Branem, A Allen

The 1960's began with the Spirit of God.. That's when the Holy Spirit began to invade the denominations and everything else. He is still invading today.. We haven't seen anything yet.

The 1970's reveal the Word of God..That is when great teachers rose up and began to reveal to us the Truth of the written Word.

The 1980's began to reveal the Prophets of God... Bob said that is when he began his ministry.

The 1990's reveal the government of God.

The 2000's will begin to reveal the Glory of God. The Glory of God is power, signs and wonders, miracles.

The 2010 will reveal the Faith of God.... Not of, but in God. What God is speaking is proclamation.. proclaiming i.. instead of begging...Going to your Daddies table and taking. We have acted like beggars and God wasn't pleased. He has set a table before us to partake in. When you begin to proclaim you loosen the Angels to go and help create. We then come to the place were we have the Faith of God.

The 2020's God begins to Rest in His church

The 2030's The family of God.. Papa is a family man and hates division in His family.

The 2040's will begin to reveal the Kingdom of God in you. Kingdom authority is when you grow up. And your Daddy turns it over to you... I think that will be your greatest testing of all time, because of the blessing that rest upon you.

Bob went home on Feb 14 2014... He believed the church would still be here through the 2050's.

Prov 12:8 A man is praised according to his wisdom,

Wisdom joins you w/grace like a covenant of marriage

Wisdom we must seek her

Faith attitude – keep your healing

Speak a creative word Isa 48:6-7

"From now on I will tell you of new things,

of hidden things unknown to you.

They are created now, and not long ago;

you have not heard of them before today.

Rom 4:17 As it is written: "I have made you a father of many nations." He is our father in the sight of God, in whom he believed-the God who gives life to the dead and calls things that are not as though they were.

2 Cor 4:13 It is written: "I believed; therefore I have spoken." With that same spirit of faith we also believe and therefore speak,

Let Christ in me "Out" You have to empty yourself

The "I" stuff can really blow the anointing!

When "I" shows up...God goes!

Many will begin to pray and seek God, not just one person!

Don't just receive the prophetic word...believe it and make it happen -

get out into the world.. His "harvest time is NOW

Using all of our 5 senses when discerning what is going on

Praying for healing

Cancer smells like musk – Sin smells unclean

Right side represents Faith

Left side represents Ministry

Don't limit God – Be determined I'm gonna see libs grow.. See the vision

Signs and Wonders are for the marketplace

Criticism – Ultimate form of pride

Turn criticism into intercession

Worse thing – running after the spectacular – DON'T DO IT

THIRTY FOUR

What is your part of the harvest?

God says "Slaves work for me – Friends work with me"

You are seated in heavenly places on the throne with Christ NOW

Speak blessings to your body. You can change your DNA

You are a new creation.

Attack against hope, family – death

Gal 5:22-23 But the fruit of the Spirit is love, joy, peace, patience, kindness, goodness, faithfulness, 23 gentleness and self-control. Against such things there is no law.

Fruit isn't works – It's relationship with Jesus

In one of the prophetic experiences that are often times given to Bob, he found himself in a Heavenly place in which he was able to observe the Lord in what seemed to be a very special day. He watched as individuals were approaching the Lord and present-ing to Him various gifts. Initially, Bob seemed a little grieved when he thought that he had come before the Lord without a gift to present. However, the Lord directed him to look at his hands and he surprisingly discovered beautiful grapes that were to be presented to the Lord as a gift.

Wondering how the grapes made their way into his possession, Bob was instructed that the grapes of Eshcol (Num 13:24 Valley of Eshcol because of the cluster of grapes)were the fruit of his decisions. During dry and difficult seasons, worldly options are presented to us. Each time we say "NO" to those options, it produced a grape that is the fruit of the promise to come... it is the sharing of the nature of Christ.

Many individuals were presenting the fruit of their journey. There were a variety of fruits presented to distinguish the various attributes they exhibited during the trying season.

"Bob's vision" people bringing fruit to the feet of the Lord. Happy birthday Jesus

large carton of oranges – Kiss the Son, peaches, apples, Bob had the small basket of big grapes.

Laid them at His feet and Jesus said "thankyou" and saw others with baskets

The only thing you can bring me is "fruit"

Every time you stand against the enemy you are bringing me fruit

This is Bob's revelation on the fruits in the basked he saw.

Orange- Representing Love. Ps 2:12- Kiss the Son, lest He be angry, and you perish in the way, when His wrath is kindled but a little. Blessed are all those who put their trust in Him.

The Lord is our great pleasure and intimacy with him produces greater expressions of love within us. This fruit can be an indication of the sun which would symbolically portray the "son."

Peach- Representing Joy. Producing a sweet sense of well-being. Pleasing to the Lord. The joy of the Lord is our strength. It is representing sweet companionship with Him.

Apple- Representing Peace. Apple has often been associated with good health. A tranquil and peaceful spirit produces a healthy body. It can also represent covenant relationship as the "Apple of His eye." Peace is generated when we are free from the anxiety and emotions of this world.

Pear-- Representing Patience. It can also be a representation of longevity. A life that is enduring without calamity.

Tomato-- Representing Kindness. The tomato is a fruit of passion representing the heart of God. It can be a symbol of "big heartedness," generosity and an undefiled conscience. This fruit can often times represent the attributes of the Lord's heart of compassion and mercy.

Strawberry-- Representing Goodness. This is a fruit symbolizing divine virtue and healing. It is often times representative of the biblical hyssop which has strong cleansing and healing components. It also can represent humility as it grows close to the ground. It is a symbol of goodness or excellence. His excellent virtue flows through us as we present ourselves in a humble state.

Grapes-- Representing Faithfulness. Grapes can be a representation of the fruit of promise. It also denotes loyalty as demonstrated by the faithful spies. Loyalty equals promises fulfilled. It is depicted when we say no to our worldly options and fears. It can also represent those who are bond-servants or "love slaves" to the Lord. John 15:15. It is a fruit sometimes illustrating friendship with the Lord.

Banana-- Representing Gentleness. The banana is softhearted and tender yet rich in nutrients. It contains vitamins essential for a healthy heart. It is also of a color that is often representative of the Glory. The amber are yellow nature of the banana can portray a representation of His Glory attributes.

Grapefruit-- Representing Self-control. It is a large citrus food that is both sweet and sour. It is sometimes difficult to endure the consequences of self-control but its fruit is "sweet." It is a representation of control in the realm of the emotions. It is sweet when it produces a focus on the Lord and sour when we are forced to deal with the nature of the old man.

2 Peter 1:5-11 For this very reason, make every effort to add to your faith goodness; and to goodness, knowledge; 6 and to knowledge, self-control; and to self-control, perseverance; and to perseverance, godliness; 7 and to godliness, brotherly kindness; and to brotherly kindness, love. 8 For if you possess these qualities in increasing measure, they will keep you from being ineffective

and unproductive in your knowledge of our Lord Jesus Christ. 9 But if anyone does not have them, he is nearsighted and blind, and has forgotten that he has been cleansed from his past sins. 10 Therefore, my brothers, be all the more eager to make your calling and election sure. For if you do these things, you will never fall, 11 and you will receive a rich welcome into the eternal kingdom of our Lord and Savior Jesus Christ.

THIRTY FIVE

This was August of 2019 We had an earthquake in Calif.
This was spoken in August 2005 in Bob's living room... Every 14 years – Shifting takes place
bondage to liberty
LA EARTHQUAKE – anytime
great shaking = great awakening
Keep taking authority over sickness. Eye of God – Father opening clockwise portal – signs in heavens.
Religious spirit: Legalism, opinion, debate, criticism, judgment

Don't blame anything that happens to you on the devil – The Lord is purifying you.
Meditate on whatever God speaks to you – an important word – let it simmer – let it take root deep down so that it will bring forth the fruit intended otherwise it will not come to pass.
The Supernatural can distract from the Word. Do not despise the small things. Keep your word – do what you say. Pray for unity – in everything. Don't take credit for God's Glory.
Ps 34:15 The eyes of the LORD are on the righteous and his ears are attentive to their cry;
Resist anxiety, fear, depression and panic. Trust in the Lord
Josh 1:5-9 No one will be able to stand up against you all the days of your life. As I was with Moses, so I will be with you; I will never leave you nor forsake you. "Be strong and courageous, because you will lead these people to inherit the land I swore to their forefathers to give them. Be strong and very courageous. Be careful to obey all the law my servant Moses gave you; do not turn from it to the right or to the left, that you may be successful wherever you

go. Do not let this Book of the Law depart from your mouth; meditate on it day and night, so that you may be careful to do everything written in it. Then you will be prosperous and successful. Have I not commanded you? Be strong and courageous. Do not be terrified; do not be discouraged, for the LORD your God will be with you wherever you go."

Do not let the enemy intimidate you – don't let him overwhelm you or wear you out.

Every conflict is the door to greater authority. Testings are meant to produce Godly character and fruit. Be Christ like in crisis

Pray for the nations... Isa 52:15 so will he sprinkle many nations, and kings will shut their mouths because of him. For what they were not told, they will see, and what they have not heard, they will understand.

God's definition of curse. It will hem you in with obstacles to bind – to render powerless – to resist what you put your hand to will not yield good fruit – it holds you back from doing what God has called you to do. Repent of delusions of grandeur

Obedience to logos produces rhema. Faith is creative

Pray for signs and wonders -gems, feathers, oil, gold and healings. Open my eyes

Stop asking – START PROCLAIMING

Popeye – keeps his eye on poppa. Protects olive oil the (anointing)

There is a fresh admonition coming from the Spirit in this hour. Many of us have become aware of the "truth" but the question is being asked... Will we live the truth? That is an all important question to determine the next level of the anointing.

THIRTY SIX

Bob would always remind us that in Rom 8:37-39 No, in all these things we are more than conquerors through him who loved us. 38 For I am convinced that neither death nor life, neither angels nor demons, neither the present nor the future, nor any powers, 39 neither height nor depth, nor anything else in all creation, will be able to separate us from the love of God that is in Christ Jesus our Lord. Paul leaves out one thing that can separate us from His Love... our PAST

In a dream Bob was told, "Those who strictly observe past glory will have little expression of present glory because they are solely focused on something that is fading."

For if that which was but passing and fading away came with splendor, how much more must that which remains and is permanent abide in glory and splendor! Since we have such [glorious] hope (such joyful and confident expectation), we speak very freely and openly and fearlessly. Nor [do we act] like Moses, who put a veil over his face so that the Israelites might not gaze upon the finish of the vanishing [splendor which had been upon it]. In fact, their minds were grown hard and calloused [they had become dull and had lost the power of understanding]; for until this present day, when the Old Testament (the old covenant) is being read, that same veil still lies [on their hearts], not being lifted [to reveal] that in Christ it is made void and done away. – 2 Corinthians 3:11-14 (Amplified)

Those who observe the fading glory of days gone by do so strictly from a misguided perspective and will have no understanding of the things that are yet to take place. Though we build upon the foundation of things that have taken place in the past, we cannot remain exclusively driven by prior expressions of outpouring and revival. There is something new and fresh on the horizon that will be a continual unfolding of the divine attributes and glory of Heaven.

Where the spirit of the Lord is, there is Liberty. We cannot allow ourselves to be content to have a retrospective point of view when the greatest glory is yet to come. The Spirit produces liberty and emancipation from the bondage of the past providing the hope of a glorious future in His rest. The Holy Spirit is currently at work equipping and supplying a body of people to live in freedom.

There is an admonition coming from the Lord highlighting our need to be more concentrated on the things that He is preparing to do rather than our adversary. Although there is merit in knowing the plans of the enemy in order to mobilize ourselves through prayer and intercession to overcome his plans, it remains imperative for us to set before us the promise of Heaven for this generation.

Our secular media has become a conduit to sow fear and intimidation into the hearts of people. Likewise, there are some misguided doomsday ministries who unfortunately overemphasize the darkness of this generation without giving adequate attention to the light that will also be delegated to a prepared and set apart people. Where darkness abounds, grace will much more abound.

The revelatory anointing resting upon God's people will allow foresight into the coming darkness. However, it also permits insight into the deposit of virtue and glory to be unleashed in unprecedented measure. We cannot allow ourselves to become overly concentrated on the darkness but exuberant with anticipation of the greatness of God to be demonstrated. Light will always overcome darkness. We are living in a time of great darkness but our directive is to be concentrated on the Light. We are to arise and shine, for our Light has come.

Bob said the Lord showed him a long golden thread – goes through all of Paul's writings – this is the priesthood of the believer.

Each of us has at least 2 angels to help us – some have more

Traditions rob us

Worship = WARship

In another prophetic encounter, Bob was told that the enemy is vigorously working to steal the "dreams" of God's people. Primarily, the dreams consist of hopes and aspirations birthed in the spirit of Christians that motivate them in prayer and set them on their prophetic journey.

In the experience, the Lord expressed that it was acceptable for His people to contemplate great and lofty things that He is capable of doing through them. That is the admonition to us in Ephesians 3:20-21—

Now to Him who is able to do exceeding abundantly beyond all that we ask or think, according to the power that works within us, to Him be the glory in the church and in Christ Jesus to all generations forever and ever. Amen.

If our dreams become exaggerated beyond the parameters of His promise, then He will make adjustments in us that keep it from becoming vain imaginations. With the vision that is being imparted to saints, there is a corresponding faith that is birthed to see it become reality. Our adversary is attempting to bring opposition to those dreams and visions with the anticipated result of birthing hopelessness and depression in its place.

Psalms 126 was given as an outline for this admonition. Those who dream in the greatness and hopeful expectation of God's restoration are filled with joy. Correspondingly, without vision, people perish in discouragement and confusion and are led into captivity.

We cannot give up the dream and aspiration of being used mightily by the Holy Spirit in the blueprint of Heaven presently being unfolded. We must also continue to dream for our children to be handed a rich spiritual inheritance.

Todays mana is tomorrows dung

You need to eat fresh mana daily!

Wanting to be someone disqualifies you

Self centeredness is the landing pad for oppression

Open Vision of sliding glass door

Heaven has doors and windows

Open heavens bring – overflowing blessings

God will speak to you if you have the intent to obey

THIRTY SEVEN

A brand new vision- a new vision but an ancient window! The Spirit of Prophecy is bringing the revelation of what Jesus is doing. We do Matthew 10:8 by Romans 10:8.

OPEN HEAVENS Deut 28:12

The LORD will open the heavens, the storehouse of his bounty, to send rain on your land in season and to bless all the work of your hands.

Heaviness will be lifted

Future prophesied and predicted

See the Lord

See Strategic purposes

Progressive revelation – who Jesus is

TO RECEIVE OPEN HEAVENS

You must be obedient Deut 28:45

Trust the Lord (tithes and offerings)

Rest in the Lord Prayer

Be heavenly minded...Phil 4:8 Finally, brothers, whatever is true, whatever is noble, whatever is right, whatever is pure, whatever is lovely, whatever is admirable-if anything is excellent or praise-worthy-think about such things

Set your affections above

God will speak to you if you have the intent to obey

If you won't obey, He won't speak to you

Testing brings you to new levels

Instant, radical obedience brings the most fruit- in finances, physical well-being, ministry

Don't give into fear or man

Obey the little tiny nudges
They are embryos of destiny
I am reminded of a brother I met with Bob
His name was Surprise from Mozambique – he visited Sudan – His was threatened
The Lord translated him to a different place at that time he had also in Mozambique
raised 53 people from the dead. Surprise can speak 15 languages. God taught him how
to speak 13 supernaturally including English.
Get rid of everything in your life – ONLY JESUS!!!
Fear of the Lord brings obedience
God does not appreciate what He does not initiate
When you come to your end...miracles begin!!!
Righteousness reveals light!!!
Hebrews 9:6-Do the deeds of Zadok. We don't get credit on earth, but if you are best known on earth, you are least known in heaven. Want to be known? The priesthood is not for ourselves...minister to the Lord and His people. Isaiah 62:6-7. Keep holding before God the promises of God. Song of Solomon 3:3; Jeremiah 31:6 and Isaiah 21.

THIRTY EIGHT

Learn to deal with panic! Don't battle panic in your thinking! Do something! Panic is when you loose your mind. Don't make deals with fear! Keep a short charge account. Deal quickly with sin! Repent daily! Keep your conscience clean so you can see! If you keep your conscience clean you will "see"! Leviticus 19:2-Holiness!" Speak to the entire assembly of Israel and say to them: 'Be holy because I, the LORD your God, am holy".

Trust-Delight-Commit-Rest-Wait-Psalm 37.

Wait on God and ask for a revelation from God.

Rom 16:20 The God of peace will soon crush Satan under your feet.

The grace of our Lord Jesus be with you.

God's peace will crush the darkness. Do not trust money or the military. God is calling for repentance! Enter the rest of faith and power. Human operation needs to cease. Salvation is the lobby of the entire building!

Do the deeds of Zadok. We don't get credit on earth, but if you are best know on earth, you are least known in heaven. Want to be known?

The priesthood isn't for ourselves – minister to the Lord and His people.

Isa 62:6-7 I have posted watchmen on your walls, O Jerusalem;they will never be silent day or night.You who call on the LORD, give yourselves no rest, and give him no rest till he establishes Jerusalem and makes her the praise of the earth. Keep holding before God the promises of God.

Song of Sol. 3:3, The watchmen found me as they made their rounds in the city.

Jer 31:6 There will be a day when watchmen cry out on the hills of Ephraim,

'Come, let us go up to Zion, to the LORD our God.'"

Isa21:6 This is what the Lord says to me: "Go, post a lookout and have him report what he sees. let him be alert, fully alert."

God doesn't appreciate what he doesn't initiate

This was spoken the day after 9/11

Ps 17:2 Let my judgment come forth from Thy presence;

Let Thine eyes look with equity.

Wake up call to a unrighteous nation,,,a wake up call to America

This is a tragedy, but no more then 10,000 abortions monthly.

IT IS A TIME FOR INTERCESSION

Rom 8:26-30

In the same way, the Spirit helps us in our weakness. We do not know what we ought to pray for, but the Spirit himself intercedes for us with groans that words cannot express. And he who searches our hearts knows the mind of the Spirit, because the Spirit intercedes for the saints in accordance with God's will. And we know that in all things God works for the good of those who love him, who have been called according to his purpose. For those God foreknew he also predestined to be conformed to the likeness of his Son, that he might be the firstborn among many brothers. And those he predestined, he also called; those he called, he also justified; those he justified, he also glorified.

Ps 102

1-7 3 months dedicated intercession

8-14 Crying out for Glory and Restoration

14-21 Glory being released

27-28 Maturing you rapidly

Relationship w/intercession - we will need to give permission for moaning and travail.

Reading the Word will change you

Titus 2:12

It teaches us to say "No" to ungodliness and worldly passions, and to live self-controlled, upright and godly lives in this present age

Insecurity can keep you out of God's plan for your life

Pray and intercede daily continually

Stop focusing on your circumstances... FOCUS ON JESUS

You have not because you ask not

Isa 58-6-14 Don't criticize !!

Turn criticism into intercession..Seek the Kingdom first

Resist fear – embrace faith and trust

Command the thief to pay back 7 times what he has stole

Receive the promises of God Psalm 91

Charlotte will be a city of refuge

The baptism of fire is a necessity

Angelic activity is increasing

To see better in the Spirit "Worship"

Pursue compassion – not power to heal

THIRTY NINE

Bob had a incredible visitation in a trance.

A man came up to him with 11 people – they were 12 angels

He said "I" am BREAKTHROUGH I was with Vincent Ioda in Nigeria (many years ago)

and I am coming to America" "I will use ordinary people – to the body of Christ

in America I say MOVE, MOVE, MOVE.

The BREAKTHROUGH is in praise and you.

2 Sam 5:17-25

17 When the Philistines heard that David had been anointed king over Israel, they went up in full force to search for him, but David heard about it and went down to the stronghold. 18 Now the Philistines had come and spread out in the Valley of Rephaim; 19 so David inquired of the LORD, "Shall I go and attack the Philistines? Will you hand them over to me?"

The LORD answered him, "Go, for I will surely hand the Philistines over to you."

20 So David went to Baal Perazim, and there he defeated them. He said, "As waters break out, the LORD has broken out against my enemies before me." So that place was called Baal Perazim. 21 The Philistines abandoned their idols there, and David and his men carried them off.

22 Once more the Philistines came up and spread out in the Valley of Rephaim; 23 so David inquired of the LORD, and he answered, "Do not go straight up, but circle around behind them and attack them in front of the balsam trees. 24 As soon as you hear the

sound of marching in the tops of the balsam trees, move quickly, because that will mean the LORD has gone out in front of you to strike the Philistine army." 25 So David did as the LORD commanded him, and he struck down the Philistines all the way from Gibeon to Gezer.

The Breakthrough angel was with David (sound of marching in the tops of the balsam trees) these are gathering angels – they will tell you what to do

We must move first – this is Conditional.

this angel spoke with Bob for 30 minutes. Vincent Ioda was with Rienhard Bonke. He raised many people from the dead, had thousands of healings and miracles took place. It was common for body parts to grow. Some meetings had over 1 million people

Let the shaking in your life bring you to seeking Him more – He is your security and peace. You have been sealed for service. Your first priority is to minister to Him.

Reading the Word will change you! Titus 2:12. It teaches us to say "No" to ungodliness and worldly passions, and to live self-controlled, upright and godly lives in this present age,

Your name means something...The Gadites - Names are attributes of God's army.

No matter how bad your thoughts are, it is not sin until you put actions to those thoughts.

DO NOT PREPARE APART FROM THE LORD!!!.

Bring your thoughts under control. Faith fuels God! You have authority over anything that touches the earth. Fear fuels the enemy...Job said "the thing that I have feared the most has come upon me". Fear breeds lust!

The baptism of fire is a necessity...Take your authority over plaques

To see in the Spirit enter into worship

Don't do deliverance alone, do it with others...

Pursue compassion – not power to heal !

When you see in dreams of a sign – Crows and blackbirds = confusion

Hawk – steals from the eagle

Eagle in America – declared no longer an endangered species (Prophetic)

Fear -self centered – not Christ centered

Corporate prayer.. Proclaim and declare

don't limit God

Renounce doubt and unbelief

It's time for signs and wonders. Call them in – miracles.

Get rid of all opinions – yield all thoughts – Ask God for His quickening – divine acceleration. It is time for Sudden happenings – everything changes

If it is inconvenient say "yes" – adjust your life

What should take years takes months

Most (pastors) spend hours with the people, and minutes with God – Nothing happens. But Jesus spent hours with God and minutes with the people and instant healings!

Intercession needs to be the foundation

The Bible promises to re-establish the judges and counselors as at the beginning that will have "butter" on their lips to convey truth and justice. (Isaiah 1:26-27) This denotes a specific anointing necessary for the articulation of kingdom truth and the pronunciation of blessings upon the righteous and judgment upon unrighteousness in the redemption of spiritual Zion.

In Isaiah 7:15 this expression is prophetically utilized to characterize the nature of the Lord's life and ministry and a time of maturing. Butter and honey will He eat until He discovers the distinction between light and darkness and learns to refuse evil and choose good. This is the ministry of extraction and separation of the mature that we are presently being called to.

But solid food is for the mature, who because of practice have their senses trained to discern good and evil. (Hebrews 5:14)

The revelation is prophetically speaking of a people coming to spiritual maturity to which a higher wisdom is imparted from the Throne of Heaven. The Zadok Priesthood portrayed in Ezekiel 44 is also a representation of the Royal Priesthood presently emerging for this divine purpose. It will be their duty to begin to separate and extract the precious from the profane...the clean from the unclean. (see Hebrews 6:1)

Those who emerge in this hour according to the characteristics described in these passages will be the ones who have "butter" on their lips to convey Heavenly wisdom and divine revelation.

FORTY

A CALL TO PRAYER

One of the warnings given to Bob Jones around December 2005 through a recent revelation has to do with the biblical balance of looking to our glorious future while also trusting God for the restoration of things lost in our past. Both are part of God's blueprint and promise; but like all spiritual principles, they must be kept in proper balance.

We are presently living in a day of restoration. The thief has set out to plunder, kill, and destroy God's people. Many seasoned Christians have been through extended battles with the adversary who has devoured finances, joy, spiritual provision and many of our promised blessings.

Even so, the Bible also affirms that the Lord will restore all that has been devoured by our adversary. (Joel 2:25) The fulfillment of that pledge is presently taking place and will escalate. Grace is being extended to plunder the enemy's camp. Nevertheless, in our pursuit to apprehend direct restoration of our inheritance, we also cannot afford to be caught in the trap of looking too intensely at the past.

Our greatest destiny and spiritual heritage is still ahead. Therefore, our counsel is to release to the Lord the issues of our past and trust Him to bring forward the restoration of our lost inheritance while at the same time focusing ardently on the glorious future promised to His people.

Matthew 13 declares that every scribe instructed in the ways of God's Kingdom, brings forth from his treasure both things old and new. That same principle applies to the appropriation of our inheritance. It will be the mingling of those things restored as well as the unprecedented release of Heaven's fresh manna.

There are great secrets of God waiting for us in the future. (Daniel 12:4) We cannot be unduly focused on the past, but faithfully trusting God and His promise to restore, in amplified ways, our lost heritage.

Bob was also given Isaiah 56:7 as a scriptural emphasis for this season.

Even those I will bring to My holy mountain and make them joyful in My house of prayer. Their burnt offerings and their sacrifices will be acceptable on My altar; for My house will be called a house of prayer for all the peoples.

God's house, His people, are to become houses of prayer. It will be through consecrated prayer that the full revelation of God's kingdom will be birthed. We need to be continued focused on our call to consecrated prayer and revelatory intercession.

We are to primarily recognize this calling and devote ourselves to it. The standard Christian life is to be a one devoted to prayer and waiting on God, however this word is a call to extraordinary prayer to launch us into the next phase of God's plan. Many people are committing several hours a day to petitioning God's Throne to birth the revelation of His kingdom in this last age. That trend will continue.

Romans 8:26-27 In the same way, the Spirit helps us in our weakness. We do not know what we ought to pray for, but the Spirit himself intercedes for us with groans that words cannot express. 27 And he who searches our hearts knows the mind of the Spirit, because the Spirit intercedes for the saints in accordance with God's will.

Psalm 102:1-7 - Three months of dedicated intercession.

8-14 - Crying out for glory and restoration.

14-21 - Glory being released.

27-28 - Maturing you rapidly.

Relationship with Intercession-We will need to give permission for moaning and travail. Reading the Word will change you! Titus 2:12. It teaches us to say "No" to ungodliness and worldly passions, and to live self-controlled, upright and godly lives in this present age,

The Gadites - Names are attributes of God's army. Means "fortune, luck"

Cancer is a rebellious cell-----one cell.

No matter how bad your thoughts are, it is not sin until you put actions to those thoughts.

DO NOT PREPARE APART FROM THE LORD!!!.

Bring your thoughts under control. Faith fuels God! You have authority over anything that touches the earth. Fear fuels the enemy...Job said "the thing that I have feared the most has come upon me". Fear breeds lust! Roman warriors look like demons or demons look like Roman warriors.

The pearl of great price is suffering!

Ex-caliber is the highest caliber-THE ANNOINTED WORD OF GOD!!!

Hebrews 5:7-The fear of the Lord. During the days of Jesus' life on earth, he offered up prayers and petitions with loud cries and tears to the one who could save him from death, and he was heard because of his reverent submission.

Jesus greatest fear was disappointing the Father. Jesus only did what He saw the Father do. He only said what he heard the Father say. Jesus' fear was a fear of not hearing and seeing the Father and then end up doing His own "stuff".

USA is having a new birth, a major change in our economy is coming. Syria is going to vanish from the face of the earth.

Isa 66:8-11 Who has ever heard of such a thing? Who has ever seen such things? Can a country be born in a day or a nation be brought forth in a moment?

Yet no sooner is Zion in labor than she gives birth to her children.

9 Do I bring to the moment of birth and not give delivery?" says the LORD.

"Do I close up the womb when I bring to delivery?" says your God.

10 "Rejoice with Jerusalem and be glad for her, all you who love her;

rejoice greatly with her, all you who mourn over her.

11 For you will nurse and be satisfied at her comforting breasts;

you will drink deeply and delight in her overflowing abundance."

The rain falls on the just and the unjust! The second fire is getting ready to start!

Discernment uses all five senses

ISA 54:11-15 O afflicted city, lashed by storms and not comforted, I will build you with stones of turquoise, your foundations with sapphires. 12 I will make your battlements of rubies, your gates of sparkling jewels, and all your walls of precious stones. 13 All your sons will be taught by the LORD, and great will be your children's peace. 14 In righteousness you will be established: Tyranny will be far from you; you will have nothing to fear. Terror will be far removed; it will not come near you. 15 If anyone does attack you, it will not be my doing; whoever attacks you will surrender to you. There has been a crushing going on.

We are becoming living stones of precious jewels

God is in the business of birthing Souls

Isa 54:1-3 "Sing, O barren woman, you who never bore a child; burst into song, shout for joy, you who were never in labor; because more are the children of the desolate woman than of her who has a husband," says the LORD. 2 "Enlarge the place of your tent, stretch your tent curtains wide, do not hold back; lengthen your cords, strengthen your stakes. 3 For you will spread out to the right and to the left; your descendants will dispossess nations and settle in their desolate cities.

Our measure of doubt destroys our measure of Faith – believe like a child – DON'T QUESTION. The enemy wants you to waver. Let Jesus be your anchor – hold on – Keep your mind on Jesus.

God is speaking to the Joshua generation (over 50 year old's) We can lead an army of youth into battle and help them cross into the promises of God.

Grow up – become Mature and take and use authority in warfare.

Intercede for America – stand in the gap

Pray against judgment

Ezek 22:30-I looked for a man among them who would build up the wall and stand before me in the gap on behalf of the land so I would not have to destroy it, but I found none.

THE FATE OF AMERICA HAS NOT YET BEEN DETERMINED – The church must stay on her knees!! Command the blessings to come !! Lust and pride are two demons over America (don't need God). Compassion for the poor and Israel is holding back severe judgement.

We the church have the authority to stop the enemy through repentance and intercession. Also break the power of his plans against your family.

THE CHURCH CAN STOP THE PLAGUES

FORTY ONE
DON'T COMPROMISE

In a vision August 31st Bob saw this: many people were imprisoned by their lost expectations. What they expected out of their lives had not come to pass.

Past disappointments or expectations for our lives have imprisoned us. **And when you look back to your past expectations, you have no vision for your future**. So our past disappointments rob us from our future vision because He's saying; I'm not disappointed in you because of your failed expectations for they were My opportunity to change your life for My purpose.

Your disappointments or expectations were stepping stones to My presence and now I'm going to demand that you flush them and look to the future not the past; for those who look to the past have no future! I now have My Spirit in many of My people.

In the vision Bob saw that many of God's saint's conscience (or their spirit) was clean but their mind wasn't. And the Holy Spirit is dealing with the mind of those that have not come to the place of where they thought they should be. Their conscience is clean and now I'm going to cleanse their soul because I'm going to use their soul and their spirit to reveal My Kingdom. So now I begin a work of cleansing their soul so their soul might be a partaker of My Divine Nature.

You're actually ready in the spirit. Now I'm preparing your soul for I'm going to use both soul and spirit. And the soul is what I'm preparing for I just want you to know that **I'm not disappointed in you and I've brought you to the place where your future in Me shall be fruit.** We must hunger after the Holy Spirit! God will justify the Spirit of Truth! Programs have replaced the Holy Spirit and compromise kills every move of God. It is though people do not have time to hunger and thirst. Hunger comes with a Godly fear. I do not want to do anything apart from the Holy Spirit. Hebrews 5:7 During the days of Jesus' life on earth, he offered up prayers and petitions with loud cries and tears to the one who could save him from death, and he was heard because of his reverent submission.
The Holy Spirit is presenting us to the Lord. The Holy Spirit presents us to Christ. The Holy Spirit is getting ready to interrupt our services if we will let him. It is not by might, nor by power, but by my Spirit says the Lord!
Additional Scriptures: Jude 20; Romans 8:26; 1st Corinthians 14:2; Ephesians 6:18.

We need to pray for the economy. Acts 3:12-19 (Amplified Bible). The law put Jesus to death and the law put the law to death and grace came forth!!!
 Hardness of heart will cause you **not** to repent. We need to see the need to repent.
 We the church have the authority to stop the enemy thru repentance and intercession.

Break the power of the enemies plans against your family

The church can stop plaques

You will eat the fruit of your lips

 Parable of Popeye

Popeye - loves olive oil (anointing)

Brutus – mind – covets the anointing

Popeye's spinach – green – the Word.. eat the spinach – Word daily
Women – "we can do it" !!

Popeye – anchor on his arm... Josh 1:8 This Book of the Law shall not depart from your mouth, but you shall meditate in it day and night, that you may observe to do according to all that is written in it. For then you will make your way prosperous, and then you will have good success.

The Joshua generation (over 50) Stand up and wage war by praising your God

Motivate and encourage the youth

We can be young at 100 years. Speak to your genetics

You need to occupy the throne room with praise (Judah) so that you can take authority. Daily give thanksgiving and praise will bring JOY

Complaining magnifies problems but Praise and thanksgiving magnifies God

 Symbols

Bear, Stagdeer – false prophets

corruption, flattery, pollution

Cat – Jezebel – lasciviousness

Excalibur sword – for the bold and brave

Sword of demacles – flattery

Giant Philistines – flesh

God wants to speak to us through His creation – birds, animals

Be a Mary – not a Martha

Obedience is the place of your provision

Expect adversity – God will help you slay the giants

1 Peter 5:10 And the God of all grace, who called you to his eternal glory in Christ, after you have suffered a little while, will himself restore you and make you strong, firm and steadfast.

Bob saw an being – "Irma"
she said it's time for women to come forth and intercede
He also saw "Charlie" – a being

He said he hasn't been on the earth since 1936. He was around with John G Lake
he was created for this time
Irma can give us direction and authority
Presumption – presuming God has told us to do something that He hasn't

FORTY TWO

SUDDENLY

Amos 9:13-15 "The days are coming," declares the LORD, "when the reaper will be overtaken by the plowman and the planter by the one treading grapes. New wine will drip from the mountains and flow from all the hills. 14 I will bring back my exiled people Israel; they will rebuild the ruined cities and live in them. They will plant vineyards and drink their wine; they will make gardens and eat their fruit. 15 I will plant Israel in their own land, never again to be uprooted from the land I have given them,"

says the LORD your God. *The Lord is giving us new weapons! The wealth of the wicked is coming to the righteous. The wicked are being brought in so they can become righteous.*

Bob saw blue leaves that were being gathered. These leaves were depicted as dry and even partially consumed to illustrate the pruning that has taken place spiritually, naturally and financially. However, once leaves have fallen there is the season for new growth which will be much more productive than in the past.

Leaves are portrayed in the Word as "healing for the nations." (Revelation 22.2) They were blue to convey the revelation of His healing grace in the various issues of life affected by the past years.

Even though this season could be depicted as a drought, many received strategic visions for the future showing productivity and prosperity through the Lord's divine favor. These revelations also outlined a blueprint for the future. The Lord is now calling us to seek Him for the provision to begin to experience and sustain the vision.

We are given the admonition to not judge the coming year by the difficulties of the prior. Very often leaves that are partially eaten or destroyed can prophetically represent worms that have had access to the leaves. The "worm" oftentimes is symbolically portrayed as our thoughts.

(Isaiah 66:24) Then they will go forth and look On the corpses of the men who have transgressed against me. For their worm will not die and their fire will not be quenched; and they will be an abhorrence to all mankind.

Our own thoughts and ways have been partially responsible for the depletion of the leaves.

We must begin to bring our thoughts into captivity and follow the leading of the Holy Spirit to gain full fruitfulness and begin to access all that is available to us in the Spirit. This will be a time of new beginnings in the coming year.

The Lord has not allowed us to be as fruitful as we would hope during this drought season because fruit that is born during drought is unsubstantial, diseased and ultimately perishes. Instead, it has been our directive to continue sowing so that the coming abundance of rain can produce a more bountiful and fruitful harvest.

(Psalm 126:3-6) The LORD has done great things for us; we are glad. Restore our captivity, O LORD, as the streams in the South-. Those who sow in tears shall reap with joyful shouting. He who goes to and fro weeping, carrying his bag of seed, shall indeed come again

with a shout of joy, bringing his sheaves with him.

Every arena of life will begin to be affected by this season of fruit-fulness. Financial, social and spiritual arenas will see a restoration that is exemplified through the Lord's healing touch. Many have experienced difficult physical and financial trials that will begin to dissipate through the "leaves of healing." Because of the challenges of this season, many Christians have withdrawn into seclusion and isolation. The Holy Spirit is encouraging us to join ourselves with others of like-mind and vision and learn to trust again. This is particularly true in marriages. It is the Lord's intent to begin to reconcile and restore strained and broken marriages produced by the adversities of past days.

There are many organizations and fellowships who have felt the direction of the Lord to expand or acquire other buildings but have seemingly been unable to fulfill the vision. This new season will now allow for the acquisition and expansion that many have felt was coming for quite some time. This will also be an indication of the fruitfulness the Church will begin to experience.

The visions providing these revelation were given on December 30, 2001. As an indication that these things are from the Holy Spirit, the Lord allowed Bob to see an ice storm that would soon be approaching as a validation of the prophetic word. Within days of releasing this message in North Carolina, an ice storm formed across the south and traveled through the eastern portion of the United States into the Carolina's doing substantial damage.

The Lord is promising that He is going to release "hail" to begin to destroy the fruit trees of Egypt. This analogy is taken from the judgement of Egypt at the time of Israel's liberation from captivity. In the areas that evil has seemingly prevailed, the Lord is going to release a form of judgement or pruning upon the spirit of this world that has prospered in unrighteousness.

(Isaiah 28:16-18) Therefore thus says the Lord GOD, "Behold, I am laying in Zion a stone, a tested stone, a costly cornerstone for the foundation, firmly placed. He who believes in it will not be disturbed. I will make justice the measuring line and righteousness the level; <u>*then hail will sweep away the refuge of lies and the waters will overflow the secret place.*</u> *Your covenant with death will be canceled, and your pact with Sheol will not stand; when the overwhelming scourge passes through, then you become its trampling place.*

Many of the difficult trials have been for the purpose of extracting issues within us as individuals that would keep us from flowing in unity as a team with others. The Lord has made it abundantly clear that He blesses those who dwell in harmony and flow together as one. Lies and talebearer wounds have successfully hindered this divine purpose. The Holy Spirit is going to expose the lies and allow truth to reign. This will also be true from the pulpits as fresh messages of Truth emerge to dispel the mists of deception and traditions of man formerly taught as truth.

Although it was difficult to discern, many people made progress in the realm of the Spirit and matured to a place in which they can be trusted with additional spiritual provision. The leaves that were demonstrated in the revelation were not fully developed nor in great abundance, but the trees did produce leaves and a measure of maturity. By virtue of this growth, many within the body will be promoted and receive greater releases of the Spirit for this next season.

The mentality for a large percentage of the Church has been placed upon survival and simply holding our ground. That mentality will now change with various leaders emerging with a warfare perspective beginning to take ground. These times have required us to dig deeper into the well of our spirit and the Holy Spirit than ever before; yet that has produced a greater foundation upon which the Lord intends to build.

Our desire is "Christ in us, the hope of glory." The Holy Spirit residing in the deep recesses of our spirit and soul will begin to lead us into the place of fruitfulness and productivity for Kingdom purposes. We are living in a new day that will be characterized by the revelation of the Lord Jesus Christ and the Kingdom which He desires to unfold within and through His people.

The Bible declares that the Lord Jesus is our ultimate example and the life He led on the earth is

our pattern. Through His Holy Spirit fully residing in us, we will also do the works He did and even greater because of His indwelling Presence. The Holy Spirit is preparing us to rule and reign with Christ in governmental authority. Governmental leadership is an aspect of His Kingdom exercising the Spiritual Dominion obtained through the cross and His resurrection.

When the Holy Spirit is resident in us, He will keep our focus on the realm of the Spirit and the Lord's overcoming victory and not the issues of this world and the distractions of carnal inclinations. When our fascination is placed upon Him, we do not see our own failures or limitations but only the abundance of His eternal ability. When we reflect on Him we do not focus on ourselves.

Lev 26:4-8 I will send you rain in its season, and the ground will yield its crops and the trees of the field their fruit. 5 Your threshing will continue until grape harvest and the grape harvest will continue until planting, and you will eat all the food you want and live in safety in your land. 6 "'I will grant peace in the land, and you will lie down and no one will make you afraid. I will remove savage beasts from the land, and the sword will not pass through your country. 7 You will pursue your enemies, and they will fall by the sword before you. 8 Five of you will chase a hundred, and a hundred of you will chase ten thousand, and your enemies will fall by the sword before you.

We need to hear for ourselves now, what part do I have in this harvest

FORTY-THREE

Time for Women and New Breed Coming Forth

Bob had a vision of angel and her name was Irma. She had a loaf of bread for women to partake and release. Joshua 1:9 don't be dismayed or discouraged -be strong and courageous.

Husbands and wives should pray together – It is more powerful than alone "if 2 or 3 agree – I'll do it. Shout out aloud your victory!! The throne of God is covered by 3 things – thunder, lighting and Shouts of God's people.

Irma and Charlie (these were two angels Bob would see often) were on the earth 6,000 years ago – creation and animals in perfect harmony. This was before Adam was created. Bob saw it all – peace on the earth. Jacob did anything and everything he could to get the anointing !! He was disparate and he got it! Irma wants to hand out fresh hot bread of anointing to women.

Negative faith is a powerful as positive faith – Watch your words!

Jesus had one fear and that was He would do something apart from His Father. Bridle your tongue – life and death is in the power of the tongue .

Over 300 doors and windows (portals) in old and new testament.

Isiah 11:11 God is giving a second chance to not only women but what he calls a "New Breed".

Bob had another vision of the new breed coming forth.

There is a coming forth of the NEW BREED! They are not old and they are not young. They will come forth in the Spirit of Holiness. *(Romans 1:4) And [as to His divine nature] according to the Spirit of holiness was openly designated the Son of God in power [in a striking, triumphant and miraculous manner] by His resurrection from the dead, even Jesus Christ our Lord (the Messiah, the Anointed One).*

The Spirit of Holiness coming forth is the divine nature of Christ. *(2 Peter 1:4-10) By means of these He has bestowed on us His precious and exceedingly great promises, so that through them you may escape [by flight] from the moral decay (rottenness and corruption) that is in the world because of covetousness (lust and greed), and become sharers (partakers) of the divine nature. For this very reason, adding your diligence [to the divine promises], employ every effort in exercising your faith to develop virtue (excellence, resolution, Christian energy), and in [exercising] virtue [develop] knowledge (intelligence), And in [exercising] knowledge [develop] self-control, and in [exercising] self-control [develop] steadfastness (patience, endurance), and in [exercising] steadfastness [develop] godliness (piety), And in [exercising] godliness [develop] brotherly affection, and in [exercising] brotherly affection [develop] Christian love. For as these qualities are yours and increasingly abound in you, they will keep [you] from being* *idle or unfruitful unto the [full personal] knowledge of our Lord Jesus Christ (the Messiah, the Anointed One). For whoever lacks these qualities is blind, [spiritually] shortsighted, seeing only what is near to him, and has become oblivious [to the fact] that he was cleansed from his old sins. Because of this, brethren, be all the more solicitous and eager to make sure (to ratify, to strengthen, to make steadfast) your calling and election; for if you do this, you will never stumble or fall.*

The new breed shall be of the divine nature and will be a friend with God. *(John 15:15) I do not call you servants (slaves) any longer; for the servant does not know what his master is doing (working out). But I have called you My friends, because I have made known to you everything that I have heard from My Father. [I have revealed to you everything that I have learned from Him.]*

The Spirit of holiness coming forth will have resurrection power in it and this power will bring the obedience of what Christ called us to. *(Matthew 10:8) cure the sick, raise the dead, cleanse the lepers, drive out demons. Freely (without pay) you have received, freely (without charge) give.*

Most of the people Bob saw were between the ages of 25 & 40. They will be the first of the new breed which others will immediately begin to follow and they will not fall back.

The Spirit of Holiness is different than the Holy Spirit although it works by the Holy Spirit. The Spirit of Holiness is the nature of Christ in you coming forth in maturity. Christ formed in you to a new level of maturity. Paul's prayer will be answered; he travailed until Christ be formed in you. *(Galations 4:19)* suffering birth pangs until Christ is formed in us.

Those who will walk forth in the Spirit of Holiness will be individuals who will represent Christ in a new level of maturity. These will be the first of the great youth leaders which countless numbers will follow.

Christ was the first of the new breed coming forth resurrected by the Spirit of Holiness. This new breed will be motivated by the Spirit of God doing nothing of themselves but only doing what they see the Father doing. *(John 5:19) so Jesus answered them by saying, I assure you, most solemnly I tell you, the Son is able to do nothing of Himself (of His own accord); but He is able to do only what He sees the Father doing, what the Son does in the same way (in His turn).*

FORTY FOUR

Bob Jones loved the Royals and the Chiefs. He told Shawn Bolz that when the Chiefs win a super bowl watch out because revival is coming. Interesting that it has been 50 years since the Chiefs were in the super bow.l.. The number 50 represents Jubilee "A fresh start". At our church today the pastor was proclaiming "It's a new day".. He knew nothing about Bob's word.... 50 is Jubilee ... Starting over clean slate

It has been a long time since I posted or talked about sports and my times with Bob.

It was Jan 2000 and the Saint Louis Rams and Tennessee Titians were to play in the Super Bowl. Bob and Viola came over to our house to watch the game. Well we all know if you don't want to know what happens don't sit next to Bob. He said Kurt Warner the quarter back was a Godly man of God, and Hwy 55 ran right through Saint Louis, so they were going to win and we would see Isa. 55 start happening. Well the Rams did win. We all were so excited. It was snowing pretty bad outside so I suggested to Bob that he and Viola stay the night. They stayed in our guest bedroom. In the morning the snow had melted enough for them to be able to go home. Well now you can't laugh at me and Janis now. After they left we were standing and looking at each other thinking about "The Prophet" stayed at our home. We ran into the guest bed room hopped on the bed and soaked up all the anointing we could....LOL

Here is his prophecy about the Kansas City Royals and Atlanta Braves....

Bob Jones' prophecy that the Kansas City Royals would be World Champs. In the spring of 1985 when Bob brought this wild and outrageous prophecy, the Royals were in the basement. People laughed and sneered at Bob calling him a false prophet, but God would prove him to be trusted and true. The Royals began to rise in the stats and go on to win the World Series against the St. Louis Cardinals.

In the fall of 2010 Bob was in a powerful trance where the Father took him to a baseball field and reminded him of past revelation. He also gave Bob understanding of the present condition of the Church and things to come. Bonnie Jones gave input also

These prophecies were parables to the Church, establishing love, faith, godly wisdom, grace and justice. After thirty years (that represents the royal priesthood), Kansas City once again holds the title of winners of "The World Series". I believe the fact that the Royals made a comeback in the 12th inning scoring 5 runs says there is grace for the royal priesthood of Believers to establish new government. And they will be the "World Champions".

Bob said he was in a high level trance; one of the highest ones that I have known in recent years. The Lord came and took me to a field and it had been covered with snow for two years. We walked out on this field and He told me to uncover a place where He pointed. So I began to rake the snow away from the place that He said, and I realized it was a **baseball plate**. I didn't rake off all of the snow I just saw it was a baseball plate. And He said, **"That's all I want you to see. This is home base and now the sun will melt the snow off of the rest of it. You did all I want you to do right now. I just wanted to show you that this is home base."**

I believe the Church is getting ready to come back to the bases.

And home base is also the beginning and the end. It's where you start, and it's also where you win. I believe that we had a start, but I think we're coming into a year of winning.

Then He said, **"Do you know what home base is?"** And I'm thinking, *No not really*. He said, "I've given you revelation in the past where home base is. But mainly home base is going to be **repentance and prayer**. These things that I've shown you in the past, I can begin to bring it in step-by-step." He said, "This field had been snowed under for two years."

So I believe the Church is going through two years of really hard, dark times. It was like we didn't know where to go, and it was like a blanket of snow was on everything. I don't think this snow meant righteousness. I think it meant two years of trouble. **These two years of trouble were coming to an end because it had accomplished some of the things it was meant to do.**

Field of Dreams

He said, "This base is international!" So I'm not speaking about one church here; I'm speaking about the Church worldwide. And He reminded me that twice before I brought a prophecy about a baseball game. Also that it reminded me of a movie called, "Field of Dreams." So I think for two years we've been plowing things under in a time of not knowing what we were doing. But we were doing our best to obey what He was telling us to do just like the *Field of Dreams*. I believe that this "Field of Dreams" is getting ready to be revealed like it was in the movie. He told me to just repeat what you did twenty-five years ago.

Kansas City Royals – 1985

On May 21st of 1985, I brought a word in Kansas City about a baseball game, and it was about the Kansas

City Royals. At that time the Kansas City Royals were then in the cellar. They hadn't won a game in quite a long while and nobody was paying much attention to them. My word was this, **"The Kansas City Royals was going to come forth and was going to begin to win. They were going to be world champions in 1985."**

This is what I saw in the vision: I saw that it was the last half of the 9th inning and satan's team was in the field and the Lord's team was at bat, and the Lord's team had two outs. **So the Lord sent in His first batter and this batter was *Love*.** So satan pitched the ball and Love swung and it was a base hit. One on.

Love is the thing that's going to be the base. Love has got to be the basis of all things in Christianity. And I believe this is the year true Christians are going to be known for the love they have for one another. True servants of the Lord. They're going to be brought into a place of loving one another to where they have total control over their tongue, over their conversation, and how they express and present things. **These three things: conversation, expression and presentation are going to be done in love. <u>There's no defense the enemy has against love.</u>**

Instead of gossip, slander, and all of these wrong things, I think that when true disciples of the Lord speak, it will be something you want to listen to. Because if they haven't got something good to say about somebody, they won't say anything. But when they're saying something good about somebody you want to hear about it, because it's going to be the truth.

So, the first batter was Love. Well, faith worketh by love. **Then the Lord sent His second batter out and His name was *Faith*.** Faith pleases God and he can't fail. So, satan pitched the ball. Faith swung. Base hit. Two on!

So, I believe the Lord is calling us to a place of faith. Faith to me is three things. Humility to me is simply being obedient to the written Word of God, the logos, for it is the law book that shows us how to grow up. And if you grow up, your conversation is going to be right. I believe there's a work in humility that I could also call obedience, but you can also call it faith.

These three things I see as one: humility, obedience, and faith.
You cannot study the Word without adding faith to it. If you obey
it, then faith is going to automatically begin to move in you because you believe the logos. Then the living Words will start coming out of you. When it does, that faith can swing and it will be a
base hit.

Then the Lord brought out His third
batter. His name was *Godly Wisdom*. And satan pitched the ball,
and Godly Wisdom looked over the ball and let it pass. Satan
pitched the second ball; He looked it over and let it pass. Satan
pitched a third ball; Godly Wisdom looked it over and also let it
pass. Then satan pitched a fourth ball; Godly Wisdom looked it
over and let it pass. **You see, <u>Godly Wisdom won't swing at what
satan is throwing at him</u>.** *(Photo via flickr)*

Many times satan throws us things and our tongue can speak it,
but Godly Wisdom won't allow it. Many times Godly Wisdom is
in our ambitions and everything, because the enemy opens doors
the Holy Spirit is not opening for us, and we enter those doors by
not discerning whether the Lord wants us to or not. We should go
to Him. **When a door opens, we should go to find out who opens
it**, and you'll know real quick-like. Is it love? Is it faith? Well, if it's
these things then it will be our witness to what the Holy Spirit's
opening. But if it's our ambition, like money, then many times the
enemy opens that door to distract us.

So Godly Wisdom looks them over and lets them all pass. Bases
loaded! And the Lord is sending in a **pinch hitter**. Nobody's ever
seen him before, and I don't think this generation has seen him.
His name is *Grace*; great Grace. So satan winds up and pitches. It
was a tremendous hit. And satan's hollering, "Don't worry about
it. I've got beelzebub (another name for satan or demon) in center

field and he's never let a fly get by." By the way, flies mean lies. And so the ball is going to center field and beelzebub is hollering, "I got it! I got it!" **But it went right through his glove and banged him in the head, and down come beelzebub. Home run! Grand slam!**

Why didn't Love, Faith, and Godly Wisdom get you through? They are only steps to prepare you for great Grace, and great Grace will get you home. The others will get you one base but great Grace will get you home!

I believe we are starting the *Season of Love*. And as we begin to love one another and be known throughout the world by the love we have for one another, we'll begin to see faith really rise up and get an answer to things. We'll begin to see the Body of Christ mature into Godly Wisdom to where we totally bridle our tongue so that when we speak, things happen. These are all a preparation for great Grace to get us home.

This was a parable of the Kansas City Royals when I brought it in 1985. They were in the cellar when I spoke this prophecy. I was pretty young in prophecy then and was really sweating it because it went all over town, and everybody said *we'd know he's a false prophet because that's not going to happen.*

Well, the Royals began to win immediately and they kept winning. They advanced to the World Series and the final game was played in Kansas City against the St. Louis Cardinals. After six games played they were tied with three games each. This was the final game of the series. And if I've ever seen a fix, Papa had a fix in on this game because the Cardinals were a powerful team, and everybody said *Kansas City doesn't stand a chance because the Cardinals are a far better team.* They had a far better coach and all the money was bet on the Cardinals.

So the game was played. It really got frustrating for the Cardinals because everything they did disintegrated, while everything the Royals did ended in home runs. It finally ended with the Royals 11 – Cardinals 0. I believe that number 11 is important because we are getting ready to start 2011.

Atlanta Braves – 1995

In 1995, I attended a MorningStar conference in Fort Mill (in South Carolina). I was living in Panama City, Florida and I was on my way up there. I was thinking of that baseball game, and that I needed to bring that prophecy again. (Paul) Keith Davis was driving me and said, "Bob, I think you ought to bring that prophecy again." I said, "That's my confirmation." When I got there, I told them I have a prophecy I want to bring and I started sharing the baseball story with them. I hadn't heard this before, but as I shared it I said, "This year it will be the Atlanta Braves," and I didn't know that till the second I spoke it. But Atlanta Braves will be the World Champions this year. So needless to say we really watched the baseball games that year.

It was the sixth game of the World Series played in Atlanta against the Cleveland Indians. The score was 0-0 going into the last half of the 9th inning and Atlanta had 2 outs, and a man by the name of David Justice comes up to the plate. He hit a home run. I believe "David's Justice" has a real meaning to it. And Atlanta was the winner that year. They became World Champions. **I believe the Lord is talking about world champions.**

World Champs – The Church

Now this is the third time I'm bringing this prophecy. He didn't tell me the name of a baseball team. There's going to be winners. I think He said the Church is the winner this year. I think the Church has sort of been in the cellar. Like literally, on our knees praying. **I think the Church is going to come out of the cellar and out of the dark place.** The cellar is dark. I think sometimes the cellar can be a comfort zone. I think we're going to come out of our comfort zone and we're going to come out into the light. And I think you're getting ready to see these four things working in the

Church this year: **Love** bringing forth **Faith**, **Godly Wisdom**, and get ready for **Grace** to come to the plate.

Home base: I think everything He's talking about is home base. Everything He's talking about here will be international – worldwide. I think we're getting ready for our Father's game to start, and I don't believe the enemy's going to be able to stop the ball from rolling. And no matter what he pitches at the Church, the Church is going to knock in a home run, because I think our Daddy has got the fix in. And I think He's appointed the Church to begin to be aware this year – to where those that don't know Him will see there's something behind these people that are representing Him.

So I think that snow has melted and the trouble is long gone. I think spring is getting ready to spring forth in the Church, and I believe you're getting ready to hear the song birds again; praise on a level like we've never heard before. I think the long, hard winter is over but the trouble in the world is only beginning. And I think the trouble in the true Church is coming to an ending, by us joining one to the other in love. **For there's no weapon the enemy's got that can defeat love. So get ready for love to be the main message you'll hear.** And you don't have to worry about the faith because if you have love it will come. Where you have that love and that faith, it will discern to where Godly Wisdom will have its way.

I believe we're in a time of tremendous change. In a time where you're going to see Christians with a smile on her face because they're going to be world winners. Get ready because you're a winner! Our old winter is gone and you're the World Champions. It's getting ready to be revealed worldwide this coming year.

FORTY FIVE

DON'T FEAR OR PANIC

What is going on today brings me back to remembering a vision and word Bob had with Paul Keith Davis.

On Aug. 7, 1998 Bob, myself and others were traveling to Mobile, Alabama for a meeting that evening. At 10 minutes before 11 a.m. the spirit of prophecy came upon Bob in a powerful way. Initially, he began to prophesy words of exhortation concerning individuals, some of which have already been fulfilled. He then began to recite "be strong and of good courage, do not fear nor be dismayed for I am with you wherever you go". Immediately I recognized that he was quoting *Joshua 1:9*. I then recalled that I had in my Bible a copy of a commission from this same passage given to a powerfully anointed prophet of the prior generation. As we began reading the commission we noticed that the Lord gave this commission by divine visitation on August 7, 1957 at 11 a.m. At approximately the same hour on the same date a commission was given out of *Joshua 1:9*.

"Have I not commanded you? Be strong and of good courage; do not be afraid, nor be dismayed, for the LORD your God is with you wherever you go." (NKJ)

The commission in 1957 immediately preceded a seven-year release of the Spirit of Revelation. This commission also marks a transition in the Spirit very similar to the change of leadership from Moses to Joshua. Even though Joshua was anointed with the spirit of Moses, he had a different ministry. A generation of mighty warriors shall soon emerge, men and women of great valor and spiritual authority like unto that of Joshua. The Lord is also going to cover us with the "shadow of His Hand", a cloud of illumination, to bring insight with understanding concerning the scriptures, especially the book of Revelation.

Only the Lord could have orchestrated the release of this commission on exactly the same date as it was given in 1957. We share these details in hopes that it will help communicate the power with which this commission came and the importance of it in the season ahead.

Subsequent to this prophecy another vision was given to Bob that emphasizes the importance of *Joshua 1:9*. In this vision Bob observed a small evil spirit whose mannerisms were similar to that of a child. In an inconsiderate manner this spirit frolicked across Bob's toes. When Bob chastised the evil spirit he saw that its name was "Anxiety". Anxiety then declared that he was going to get his father to deal with Bob.

As this smaller spirit returned Bob saw that his gigantic father came with him. This spirit was seemingly 50 feet tall and was named "Panic". Panic had just returned from killing 1,000 people that day and threatened to do the same to Bob if he chastised "anxiety" again. Bob knew that if the Lord did not intervene, panic was capable of making good on his promise. Panic then retrieved his cousin named "Thief" and together they intended to destroy Bob and steal his goods.

When fear and panic seemed that they were going to overwhelm him, Bob heard the Holy Spirit say "why don't you call the law on these thieves". Bob then went to the telephone and instead of dialing 9-1-1, he dialed 1-0-1-9—*Luke 10:19*.

"Behold, I have given you authority to tread upon serpents and scorpions, and over all the power of the enemy, and nothing shall injure you. (NAS)

Not only did the law shackle anxiety, panic, and the thief, the law also required a seven-fold return of all that had been stolen.

Anxiety and panic have gripped the world and even many in the church. One of the signs of the last days is that men's hearts will fail them for fear. These evil spirits rob the people of God of their peace and joy and impart fear, the greatest enemy of our faith. The Lord is commanding us to be strong and of good courage for He is imparting the reality of *Luke 10:19*. Because of the great victory of the cross we need not fear nor be dismayed for the Lord has delegated to us His authority over all the power of the enemy.

The Lord is going to anoint His people with courage and valor to demonstrate to the world His dominion over fear and panic and all the power of the evil one. A courageous generation with resolute determination and anointing shall arise to uproot the enemies of the Faith that have kept us from the Promises of God. Once the Church takes it rightful position in the "promised land" the Glory of God will shine upon her as a testimony to the whole Earth of God's salvation and deliverance.

God be gracious to us and bless us, {and} cause His face to shine upon us, Selah. That Thy way may be known on the earth, Thy salvation among all nations. God blesses us, that all the ends of the earth may fear Him. (NAS) Psalms 67:1-2, 7

FORTY SIX

BE STRONG AND OF GOOD COURAGE

Bob had revelations about the important commissioning of Joshua following the death of Moses. The admonition came from Joshua 1:9. And Deuteronomy 9:1

Have I not commanded you? Be strong and of good courage; do not be afraid, nor be dismayed, for the LORD your God is with you wherever you go. (Joshua 1:9)

Hear, O Israel! You are crossing over the Jordan today to go in to dispossess nations greater and mightier than you, great cities fortified to heaven (Deuteronomy 9:1)

A DANGEROUS TIME

The Holy Spirit spoke to Bob and indicated that this is a dangerous time, but His champions are willing to live "dangerously." Note, however, this is not saying to live carelessly or presumptuously... only that we be willing to trust the Lord and take a chance on Him. Israel trusted the counsel of Heaven in taking Jericho, although the instruction seemed foolish and dangerous. Their obedience facilitated great victory.

This will be a season to try new things and even be willing to "walk in the lion's den", if so directed. In Daniel's obedience and service to the Lord, he found himself thrust into a dangerous situation among a den of lions. Nonetheless, he was covered and protected and witnessed the provision of Heaven because of the righteousness of his heart.

THE SUDDENLIES OF HEAVEN

At 5:08 AM a further instruction was given to Bob related to the "suddenlies" of Heaven. Although things may seem difficult and trying, they can suddenly change. Perhaps there have been promises and visions given to some that have seemingly died on the vine. However, they can abruptly come to life and become reality.

Bob also heard a unique expression, especially for someone not electronically oriented. It was, "laptops will now come alive." The Holy Spirit seems to be pointing to a distinguished anointing upon the writing of Biblical truth and spiritual reality. This would not be limited to books and articles but also creative expressions of songs, poetry and other means of Communicating Truth.

THE SPIRIT OF RESTORATION

On the morning of Pentecost I also received a dream in which an ancient sword was being restored. It was one of great value and prominence but had been lost and only recently excavated. Our sword of the Spirit is the Word of God.

Although this newly found sword bore the evidence of being buried, it was immediately put to use upon discovery. With it, we were able to eliminate nocturnal predators, devourers and other unclean adversaries.

My heart overflows with a good theme; I address my verses to the King; My tongue is the pen of a ready writer. Thou art fairer than the sons of men; Grace is poured upon Thy lips; therefore God has blessed Thee forever. Gird Thy sword on Thy thigh, O Mighty One, in Thy splendor and Thy majesty! And in Thy majesty ride on victoriously, for the cause of truth and meekness and righteousness; let Thy right hand teach Thee awesome things. (Psalm 45:1-4)

This seemed to also point to both the spoken and written word utilized by the Holy Spirit to expose and neutralize adversaries previously successful in devouring and stealing seeds of promise and purpose.

FORTY SEVEN

Thinking about when I used to sit at Bob's feet and listen to him encourage us in the Lord.

Let your vision be enlarged..God has given us dominion...We need to take authority to reestablish His Kingdom on earth.

We need to take authority over our own storms- bind and rebuke Once you have seen and experienced God moving in a area you must rise to that level and believe for the same results in a similar circumstance or trial – Total Faith

There are six hindrances

1. Disobedience 2. Unforgiveness 3. Compromise "the enemy has nothing in me"

4. Not submitting to the Lordship of Christ in you life. 5. Heart is divided 6. Settling for less

Take authority against all sickness and disease in you and your families life

Receive the mantle of Kingdom dominion and authority

Ps. 91 "under the shadow of Your wings I will take refuge – promise of protection"

Your mind is your livingroom – keep it clean – let go of the past. Seared conscience – no conviction of sin..Greatest sin of the Body of Christ is losing our first love – holding on to grievances to disappointments the past – talk about Him Eph2:22 You're the dwelling place

Ps. 34:15 eyes of the Lord upon the righteous, and His ears are open to their cry. Anything is possible!! Speak it out. Our words can create miracles! Jer 29:13 You will find Me when ou search with all your heart.

God hides Himself in inconveniences

1. Obedience – hear with intent to obey..God doesn't speak sometimes, because He knows we won't obey and then He would have to discipline us for not doing what He asks.

2. Manna – daily provision – not for tomorrow - Economy of heaven no lack

Generosity – giving above and beyond...

Your mind is a open field and launching to the heavenly or demonic realm. It is a battle.

You must empower the heavenly realm

Have a warrior spirit – take dominion – Pray in tongues for hours

Believe miracles will come

Praise is key to victory!

Worship at your most difficult times is the most precious to God

Don't run ahead of God – Wait on Him

Soaking – drawing aside to be with Him on a regular basis – resting

Distraction destroys your focus, Speaking in tongues – is lake a baby nursing on it's mother,

We nurse from the Many Breasted One –(El Shadday) receiving spiritual milk- which is living tissue

FORTY EIGHT

Obey God and serve God with joy

Deut 28:1- If you fully obey the LORD your God and carefully follow all his commands I give you today, the LORD your God will set you high above all the nations on earth. 2 All these blessings will come upon you and accompany you if you obey the LORD your God:

Deut 28:47 Because you did not serve the LORD your God joyfully and gladly in the time of prosperity

Endurance – faith sustained over time in the midst of pain, holding on to hope with patience

James 5:7-11 Be patient, then, brothers, until the Lord's coming. See how the farmer waits for the land to yield its valuable crop and how patient he is for the autumn and spring rains. 8 You too, be patient and stand firm, because the Lord's coming is near. 9 Don't grumble against each other, brothers, or you will be judged. The Judge is standing at the door!

10 Brothers, as an example of patience in the face of suffering, take the prophets who spoke in the name of the Lord. 11 As you know, we consider blessed those who have persevered. You have heard of Job's perseverance and have seen what the Lord finally brought about. The Lord is full of compassion and mercy.

As a man thinks in his heart, so he is

accusation – seed of oppression

"do not fear the fiery darts of the enemy. Just dive into God's river and you will not be burned" Put on an over coming spirit

Deep repentance is the spiritual toilet..it cleanses from all defilement

sometimes it looks like a person has died young- before their time, but God says, "it was their time to go – their destiny and purpose could only be completed and fulfilled in heaven.

Bob heard an angel say "Wake up" "Stop going thru the motions. Get intimate with Jesus. It's a choice. Have an undivided heart."

The same area that you have been attacked in the most (finances, ministry) will be the same area that you be blessed in the most.

Your thoughts will empower with light or darkness-giving into frustration or bitterness reduces your spiritual effectiveness

The first hour of your day is the most important – Command Kingdom Come in your home daily.

The enemy tries to suppress us daily – it is a daily battle – we are to advance the governmental of God's Kingdom continually on a daily basis

Do not get stuck the wilderness of the world – the way we live empowers the kingdom of light or darkness. We must not be complacent or apathetic – we need to walk in a warrior spirit to advance God's kingdom

Proclamations are stronger than intercession

FORTY NINE

Love is the pearl of great price. We have Jesus DNA and genetics containing all of God's kingdom. We can take authority and change our DNA.

Put God in remembrance of His promises.

Attitude determines altitude. Replace negative thought patterns with positive biblical confessions.

The harder you try to see and hear in the spirit realm – the less you will be able to. The more your try to grasp it the less it will happen. Rest and receive – Let go

What your imagination sees determines what your life will be like.

Your spiritual walk is determined by the state of your mind.

The following are nuggets were from my journey in healing of my body.

THE LORD IS COMMITTED TO US BECOMING A TESTIMONY IN THE EARTH

The Lord wants me to be a testimony

Luke 12:8

"And I say to you, everyone who confesses Me before men, the Son of Man shall confess him also before the angels of God; HE IS THE WORD

Romans 10:8-11

But what does it say? "THE WORD IS NEAR YOU, in your mouth and in your heart"-- that is, the word of faith which we are preaching, 9that if you confess with your mouth Jesus as Lord, and believe in your heart that God raised Him from the dead, you shall be saved; 10for with the heart man believes, resulting in righteousness, and with the mouth he confesses, resulting in salvation. 11For the Scripture says, "WHOEVER BELIEVES IN HIM WILL NOT BE DISAPPOINTED."

2 Cor. 4:13-15

But having the same spirit of faith, according to what is written, "I BELIEVED, THEREFORE I SPOKE," we also believe, therefore also we speak; 14knowing that He who raised the Lord Jesus will raise us also with Jesus and will present us with you. 15For all things are for your sakes, that the grace which is spreading to more and more people may cause the giving of thanks to abound to the glory of God.

2 Cor. 4:16-18

Therefore we do not lose heart, but though our outer man is decaying, yet our inner man is being renewed day by day. 17For momentary, light affliction is producing for us an eternal weight of glory far beyond all comparison, 18while we look not at the things which are seen, but at the things which are not seen; for the things which are seen are temporal, but the things which are not seen are eternal.

Romans 4:18-21

In hope against hope he believed, in order that he might become a father of many nations, according to that which had been spoken, "SO SHALL YOUR DESCENDANTS BE." 19And without becoming weak in faith he contemplated his own body, now as good as dead since he was about a hundred years old, and the deadness of Sarah's womb; 20yet, with respect to the promise of God, he did not waver in unbelief, but grew strong in faith, giving glory to God, 21and being fully assured that what He had promised, He was able also to perform.

TRUTH IS ABOVE REALITY

1 John 3:1-3

See how great a love the Father has bestowed upon us, that we should be called children of God; and such we are. For this reason the world does not know us, because it did not know Him. 2Beloved, now we are children of God, and it has not appeared as yet what we shall be. We know that, when He appears, we shall be like Him, because we shall see Him just as He is. 3And everyone who has this hope fixed on Him purifies himself, just as He is pure.

LET'S BELIEVE GOD

Rom 10:17 So then faith comes by hearing, and hearing by the word of God.

WHEN YOU READ THE BIBLE.. LISTEN

Genesis 18:14 "Is anything too difficult for the LORD?

Jeremiah 32:27 Behold, I am the LORD, the God of all flesh: is there any thing too hard for me?

Matthew 19:26 And looking upon them Jesus said to them, "With men this is impossible, but with God all things are possible."

Luke 1:37 For nothing will be impossible with God."

Mark 11:22-24   HAVE=TO TAKE HOLD OF

And Jesus answered saying to them, "Have faith in God. 23"Truly I say to you, whoever says to this mountain, 'Be taken up and cast into the sea,' and does not doubt in his heart, but believes that what he says is going to happen, it shall be granted him. 24"Therefore I say to you, all things for which you pray and ask, believe that you have received them, and they shall be granted you.

Hebrews 6:17-19

In the same way God, desiring even more to show to the heirs of the promise the unchangeableness of His purpose, interposed with an oath, 18in order that by two unchangeable things, in which it is impossible for God to lie, we may have strong encouragement, we who have fled for refuge in laying hold of the hope set before us. 19This hope we have as an anchor of the soul, a hope both sure and steadfast and one which enters within the veil,

Hebrews 11:1-8 Now faith is being sure of what we hope for and certain of what we do not see. 2This is what the ancients were commended for.

2 Cor. 4:13-18 But having the same spirit of faith, according to what is written, "I BELIEVED, THEREFORE I SPOKE," we also believe, therefore also we speak; 14knowing that He who raised the Lord Jesus will raise us also with Jesus and will present us with you. 15For all things are for your sakes, that the grace which is spreading to more and more people may cause the giving of thanks to abound to the glory of God. 16Therefore we do not lose heart, but though our outer man is decaying, yet our inner man is being renewed day by day. 17For momentary, light affliction is producing for us an eternal weight of glory far beyond all comparison, 18while we look not at the things which are seen, but at the things which are not seen; for the things which are seen are temporal, but the things which are not seen are eternal.

Rom 4:17"I have made you a father of many nations." He is our father in the sight of God, in whom he believed-the God who gives life to the dead and calls things that are not as though they were.

HOW DO WE PRESS IN TO GOD'S FAITH

Rom 10:17 So then faith comes by hearing, and hearing by the word of God.

WHEN WE READ THE BIBLE.. LISTEN

Matthew 5:6 Blessed are those who hunger and thirst for righteousness, for they will be filled.

Philip. 3:14 I press on toward the goal to win the prize for which God has called me heavenward in Christ Jesus

Psalm 63:1-11

God, you are my God, earnestly I seek you;my soul thirsts for you my body longs for you,in a dry and weary land where there is no water. 2I have seen you in the sanctuary and beheld your power and your glory. 3Because your love is better than life,my lips will glorify you.I will praise you as long as I live,and in your name I will lift up my hands. 5My soul will be satisfied as with the richest of foods;with singing lips my mouth will praise you. 6On my bed I remember you; think of you through the watches of the night.7 Because you are my help,I sing in the shadow of your wings. 8My soul clings to you; your right hand upholds me. 9They who seek my life will be destroyed;they will go down to the depths of the earth. 10They will be given over to the sword and become food for jackals.11But the king will rejoice in God;all who swear by God's name will praise him,while the mouths of liars will be silenced.

Proverbs 8:17 I love them that love me; and those that seek me early shall find me.

Col. 3:1-17 If then you have been raised up with Christ, keep seeking the things above, where Christ is, seated at the right hand of God. 2Set(SETTLE IT) your mind on the things above, not on the things that are on earth. 3For you have died and your life is hidden with Christ in God. 4When Christ, who is our life, is revealed, then you also will be revealed with Him in glory.

5Therefore consider the members of your earthly body as dead to immorality, impurity, passion, evil desire, and greed, which amounts to idolatry. 6For it is on account of these things that the wrath of God will come, 7and in them you also once walked, when you were living in them. 8But now you also, put them all aside: anger, wrath, malice, slander, and abusive speech from your mouth. 9Do not lie to one another, since you laid aside the old self with its evil practices, 10and have put on the new self who is being renewed to a true knowledge according to the image of the One who created him 11a renewal in which there is no distinction between Greek and Jew, circumcised and uncircumcised, barbarian, Scythian, slave and freeman, but Christ is all, and in all.

12And so, as those who have been chosen of God, holy and beloved, put on a heart of compassion, kindness, humility, gentleness and patience; 13bearing with one another, and forgiving each other, whoever has a complaint against anyone; just as the Lord forgave you, so also should you. 14And beyond all these things put on love, which is the perfect bond of unity. 15And let the peace of Christ rule in your hearts, to which indeed you were called in one body; and be thankful. 16Let the word of Christ richly dwell within you, with all wisdom teaching and admonishing one another with psalms and hymns and spiritual songs, singing with thankfulness in your hearts to God. 17And whatever you do in word or deed, do all in the name of the Lord Jesus, giving thanks through Him to God the Father.

Prov 4:20-22 My son, pay attention to what I say; listen closely to my words.

 Do not let them out of your sight, keep them within your heart; for they are life to those who find them and health to a man's whole body.

FIGHTING THE GOOD FIGHT...THE ONE THAT WE WIN

James 1:2-4

Consider it pure joy, my brothers, whenever you face trials of many kinds, 3because you know that the testing of your faith develops perseverance. 4Perseverance must finish its work so that you may be mature and complete, not lacking anything.

1 Tim. 6:12

Fight the good fight of faith; take hold of the eternal life to which you were called, and you made the good confession in the presence of many witnesses.   THE WORD CONFESSION MEANS AAGREEMENT@

2 Cor. 4:13-14

But having the same spirit of faith, according to what is written, "I BELIEVED, THEREFORE I SPOKE," we also believe, therefore also we speak; 14knowing that He who raised the Lord Jesus will raise us also with Jesus and will present us with you.

John 6:29

Jesus answered and said to them, "This is the work of God, that you believe in Him whom He has sent."

John 1:12-13

12 Yet to all who received him, to those who believed in his name, he gave the right(Power) to become children of God- children born not of natural descent, nor of human decision or a husband's will, but born of God.

2 Cor 5:17

17 Therefore, if anyone is in Christ, he is a new creation; the old has gone, the new has come!

Rom 8:31-32

31 What, then, shall we say in response to this? If God is for us,

who can be against us? 32 He who did not spare his own Son, but gave him up for us all-how will he not also, along with him, graciously give us all things?

I can do everything through him who gives me strength.

Phil 4:4-10

4 Rejoice in the Lord always. I will say it again: Rejoice! 5 Let your gentleness be evident to all. The Lord is near .Do not be anxious about anything, but in everything, by prayer and petition, with thanksgiving, present your requests to God. 7 And the peace of God, which transcends all understanding, will guard your hearts and your minds in Christ Jesus8 Finally, brothers, whatever is true, whatever is noble, whatever is right, whatever is pure, whatever is lovely, whatever is admirable-if anything is excellent or praiseworthy-think about such things. 9 Whatever you have learned or received or heard from me, or seen in me-put it into practice. And the God of peace will be with you.

Phil 4:11-12

11 I am not saying this because I am in need, for I have learned to be content whatever the circumstances. I know what it is to be in need, and I know what it is to have plenty or want. I can do everything through him who gives me strength.

1 Peter 1:3-9

Grace and peace be yours in abundance.

3 Praise be to the God and Father of our Lord Jesus Christ! In his great mercy he has given us new birth into a living hope through the resurrection of Jesus Christ from the dead, and into an inheritance that can never perish, spoil or fade-kept in heaven for you, who through faith are shielded by God's power until the coming

of the salvation that is ready to be revealed in the last time. In this you greatly rejoice, though now for a little while you may have had to suffer grief in all kinds of trials. These have come so that your faith-of greater worth than gold, which perishes even though refined by fire-may be proved genuine and may result in praise, glory and honor when Jesus Christ is revealed. Though you have not seen him, you love him; and even though you do not see him now, you believe in him and are filled with an inexpressible and glorious joy, 9 for you are receiving the goal of your faith, the salvation of your souls.

Heb 1:13-14

13 To which of the angels did God ever say,

"Sit at my right hand until I make your enemies a footstool for your feet"?

14 Are not all angels ministering spirits sent to serve those who will inherit salvation?

Josh 1:2-5

Moses my servant is dead. Now then, you and all these people, get ready to cross the Jordan River into the land I am about to give to them-to the Israelites. 3 I will give you every place where you set your foot, as I promised Moses. 4 Your territory will extend from the desert to Lebanon, and from the great river, the Euphrates-all the Hittite country-to the Great Sea on the west. 5 No one will be able to stand up against you all the days of your life. As I was with Moses, so I will be with you; I will never leave you nor forsake you.

Prov 8:17-21

17 I love those who love me,and those who seek me find me. 18

With me are riches and honor, enduring wealth and prosperity. 19 My fruit is better than fine gold;what I yield surpasses choice silver. 20 I walk in the way of righteousness,along the paths of justice,

21 bestowing wealth on those who love me and making their treasuries full.

1 Peter 5:6-11

Humble yourselves, therefore, under the mighty hand of God, that He may exalt you at the proper time, 7casting all your anxiety upon Him, because He cares for you. 8Be of sober spirit, be on the alert. Your adversary, the devil, prowls about like a roaring lion, seeking someone to devour. 9But resist him, firm in your faith, knowing that the same experiences of suffering are being accomplished by your brethren who are in the world. 10And after you have suffered for a little while, the God of all grace, who called you to His eternal glory in Christ, will Himself perfect, confirm, strengthen and establish you. 11To Him be dominion forever and ever. Amen.

Col. 3:1-3

If then you have been raised up with Christ, keep seeking the things above, where Christ is, seated at the right hand of God. 2Set (settle it) your mind on the things above, not on the things that are on earth. 3For you have died and your life is hidden with Christ in God.

2 Cor 4:16-18

16 Therefore we do not lose heart. Though outwardly we are wasting away, yet inwardly we are being renewed day by day. 17 For our light and momentary troubles are achieving for us an

eternal glory that far outweighs them all. 18 So we fix our eyes not on what is seen, but on what is unseen. For what is seen is temporary, but what is unseen is eternal.

Heb 5:13-14

14 But solid food belongs to those who are of full age, that is, those who by reason of use have their senses exercised to discern both good and evil.

Prov 8:34-35

34 Blessed is the man who listens to me, watching daily at my doors, waiting at my doorway. 35 For whoever finds me finds life and receives favor from the LORD.

Psalm 68:1

Let God arise, let His enemies be scattered; And let those who hate Him flee before Him.

GOING THROUGH MY TRIAL

Pro 3:6 In all my ways acknowledge Him, and He shall direct my paths...

I want to walk in His foot steps....

EPH 2:6 Because of Christ's resurrection, we know that our bodies will also be raised from the dead (1 Cor. 15:2 23) and that we have been given the power to live as Christians now (1:19). These ideas are combined in Paul's image of sitting with Christ in "the heavenly realms" (see the note on 1:3). Our eternal life with Christ is certain because we are united in his powerful victory.1 THESS 5:16 18 Our joy, prayers, and thankfulness should not fluctuate with our circumstances or feelings. Obeying these three commands be joyful, pray continually, and give thanks often goes against our natural inclinations. When we make a conscious decision to do what God says, however, we will begin to see people in a new perspective. When we do God's will, we will find it easier to be joyful and thankful.

1 THESS 5:17 We cannot spend all our time on our knees, but it is possible to have a prayerful attitude at all times. This attitude is built upon acknowledging our dependence on God, realizing his presence within us, and determining to obey him fully. Then we will find it natural to pray frequent, spontaneous, short prayers. A prayerful attitude is not a substitute for regular times of prayer but should be an outgrowth of those times.

1 THESS 5:18 Paul was not teaching that we should thank God [for] everything that happens to us, but]in] everything. Evil does not come from God, so we should not thank him for it. But when evil strikes, we can still be thankful for God's presence and for the good that he will accomplish through the distress.

PHIL 4:10 14 Are you content in any circumstances you face? Paul knew how to be content whether he had plenty or whether he was in need. The secret was drawing on Christ's power for strength. Do you have great needs, or are you discontented because you don't have what you want? Learn to rely on God's promises and Christ's power to help you be content. If you always want more, ask God to remove that desire and teach you contentment in every circumstance. He will supply all your needs, but in a way that he knows is best for you (see the note on 4:19 for more on God supplying our needs).

PHIL 4:12, 13 Paul was content because he could see life from God's point of view. He focused on what he was supposed to [do,] not what he felt he should]have.] Paul had his priorities straight, and he was grateful for everything God had given him. Paul had detached himself from the nonessentials so that he could concentrate on the eternal. Often the desire for more or better possessions is really a longing to fill an empty place in a person's life. To what are you drawn when you feel empty inside? How can you find true contentment? The answer lies in your perspective, your priorities, and your source of power.

PHIL 4:13 Can we really do everything? The power we receive in union with Christ is sufficient to do his will and to face the challenges that arise from our commitment to doing it. He does not grant us superhuman ability to accomplish anything we can imagine without regard to his interests. As we contend for the faith we will face troubles, pressures, and trials. As they come, ask Christ to strengthen you.

PHIL 2:12 "Therefore" ties this verse to the previous section. "Work out your salvation," in light of the preceding exhortation to unity, may mean that the entire church was to work together to rid themselves of divisions and discord. The Philippian Christians needed to be especially careful to obey Christ, now that Paul wasn't there to continually remind them about what was right. We too must be careful about what we believe and how we live, especially when we are on our own. In the absence of cherished Christian leaders, we must focus our attention and devotion even more on Christ so that we won't be sidetracked.

PHIL 2:13 What do we do when we don't feel like obeying? God has not left us alone in our struggles to do his will. He wants to come alongside us and be within us to help. God helps us [want] to obey him and then gives us the]power] to do what he wants. The secret to a changed life is to submit to God's control and let him work. Next time, ask God to help you]want] to do his will.

PHIL 2:13 To be like Christ, we must train ourselves to think like Christ. To change our desires to be more like Christ's, we need the power of the indwelling Spirit (1:19), the influence of faithful Christians, obedience to God's Word (not just exposure to it), and sacrificial service. Often it is in]doing] God's will that we gain the]desire] to do it (see 4:8, 9). Do what he wants and trust him to change your desires.

PHIL 2:14 16 Why are complaining and arguing so harmful? If all that people know about a church is that its members constantly argue, complain, and gossip, they get a false impression of Christ and the gospel. Belief in Christ should unite those who trust him. If your church is always complaining and arguing, it lacks the unifying power of Jesus Christ. Stop arguing with other Christians or complaining about people and conditions within the church and let the world see Christ.

PHIL 2:14 16 Our lives should be characterized by moral purity, patience, and peacefulness, so that we will "shine like stars" in a dark and depraved world. A transformed life is an effective witness to the power of God's Word. Are you shining brightly, or are you clouded by complaining and arguing? Shine out for God.

PHIL 2:17 The drink offering was an important part of the sacrificial system of the Jews (for an explanation, see Numbers 28:7). Because this church had little Jewish background, the drink offering may refer to the wine poured out to pagan deities prior to important public events. Paul regarded his life as a sacrifice.

PHIL 2:17 Even if he had to die, Paul was content, knowing that he had helped the Philippians live for Christ. When you're totally committed to serving Christ, sacrificing to build the faith of others brings a joyous reward.

2 COR 4:8 12 Paul reminds us that though we may think we are at the end of the rope, we are never at the end of hope. Our perishable bodies are subject to sin and suffering, but God never abandons us. Because Christ has won the victory over death, we have eternal life. All our risks, humiliations, and trials are opportunities for Christ to demonstrate his power and presence in and through us.

2 Corinthians :15 18 Paul had faced sufferings, trials, and distress as he preached the Good News. But he knew that they would one day be over, and he would obtain God's rest and rewards. As we face great troubles, it's easy to focus on the pain rather than on our ultimate goal. Just as athletes concentrate on the finish line and ignore their discomfort, we too must focus on the reward for our faith and the joy that lasts forever. No matter what happens to us in this life, we have the assurance of eternal life, when all suffering will end and all sorrow will flee away (Isaiah 35:10).

ROMANS 10:8 11   SOMETHING REALLY HAPPENS WHEN WE CONFESS THE TRUTH.

2 COR 4:13 14 WHAT ARE GOING AROUND SPEAKING.. WHERE IS OUR FAITH POINT TOO.

I want to see

1 John 3:1

See how great a love the Father has bestowed on us, that we would be called children of God; and such we are.

Eph 2:6 And God raised us up with Christ and seated us with him in the heavenly realms in Christ Jesus,

Rev 21:1-8

21:1 Then I saw a new heaven and a new earth, for the first heaven and the first earth had passed away, and there was no longer any sea. 2 I saw the Holy City, the new Jerusalem, coming down out of heaven from God, prepared as a bride beautifully dressed for her husband. 3 And I heard a loud voice from the throne saying, "Now the dwelling of God is with men, and he will live with them. They will be his people, and God himself will be with them and be their God. 4 He will wipe every tear from their eyes. There will be no more death or mourning or crying or pain, for the old order of things has passed away."

5 He who was seated on the throne said, "I am making everything new!" Then he said, "Write this down, for these words are trustworthy and true."

6 He said to me: "It is done. I am the Alpha and the Omega, the Beginning and the End. To him who is thirsty I will give to drink without cost from the spring of the water of life. 7 He who overcomes will inherit all this, and I will be his God and he will be my son.

Heb 4:10-11 for anyone who enters God's rest also rests from his own work, just as God did from his. 11 Let us, therefore, make every effort to enter that rest, so that no one will fall by following their example of disobedience.